Blessi

Blessing the Church?

A review of the history and direction of the charismatic movement

Clifford Hill
Peter Fenwick
David Forbes
David Noakes

Guildford, Surrey

British Library Cataloguing in Publication Data. A catalogue record for this book is available from the British Library.

Published by Eagle, an imprint of Inter Publishing Service (IPS) Ltd, St Nicholas House, 14 The Mount, Guildford, Surrey GU2 5HN.

Phototypeset by Intype, London

Printed by HarperCollins, Glasgow

ISBN No: 0 86347 186 2

Contents

CHAPTER ONE

INTRODUCTION

Few observers of the church scene would deny that the 1990s have proved to be a critical period for the charismatic movement. The publication of books and articles speaking about a crisis within the movement has proliferated. Hank Hanegraaff in *Christianity in Crisis*[1] has carried out extensive research of the teaching given by a number of prominent charismatic leaders. He has looked at their statements in comparison with Scripture and found that many of them are contrary to the Bible. There is growing anxiety, not simply among reformed evangelicals, but among many within the charismatic movement concerning a serious drift away from biblical principles. Of course, there will always be differences of interpretation and textual exegesis. But differences in interpretation cannot account for statements which are directly contrary to those found in the Bible.

The charismatic movement has been a tremendous blessing to millions of Christians who have found a new freedom in worship and a deeper personal relationship with God which has strengthened their faith and enabled them to participate more actively in the work of the gospel. The emphasis upon personal experience which broke the icy grip of traditionalism in most branches of the church has also had its down side as charismatics have been carried along on waves of excitement into deeper realms of experience. Any movement or teaching which offers the believer a deeper personal experience with the living God is highly attractive. Yet when experience parts company with sound biblical teaching there is grave danger for the believer. There is strong evidence that this is what has been happening within the charismatic movement.

The Toronto Blessing

The latest wave of spiritual experience known as the Toronto Blessing has received worldwide publicity. In Britain a number of books were on the market within months of the first appearance of the phenomenon. These offered uncritical and excited accounts of what was variously described as revival, pre-revival, times of refreshing, the impartation of supernatural power and numerous other descriptions.

There were many published accounts of the benefits of the 'blessing' in the lives of believers. Many testified that they had been drawn into closer communion with God, a deeper commitment to prayer, to Bible study and renewed love for Jesus. At the same time there were many accounts of bizarre phenomena such as making animal noises and uncontrollable physical manifestations including screaming and vomiting which many charismatics did not believe could be the work of the Holy Spirit. At the height of the Toronto Blessing many churches gave scant attention to the preaching and expounding of the Word of God. In some cases this was enforced due to the preacher becoming overcome by physical convulsions which rendered him incapable of speech. Many charismatics shook their heads and said surely God would not hinder the proclamation of his own Word! Others were greatly excited by these strange activities and participated enthusiastically in the 'receiving meetings' where the emphasis was upon receiving 'more of God'.

Divisive Effect

In Britain, the Toronto Blessing resulted in the most widespread and deep-rooted division to hit the church for many years. This division was not between believers and unbelievers, or between evangelical and liberal; it was a division among charismatics themselves. It brought division in the families of believers, it divided prayer groups, it brought division and splits within congregations and it divided church from church even within the same denomination.

There is evidence of thousands of Spirit-filled believers leaving their churches and being forced to seek other places of worship or simply meeting in little ad hoc house fellowships, or even going nowhere while nursing the hurts of rejection by leaders who refused to hear any questioning of the bizarre activities in their congregation. This division contrasts strangely with the experience of the disciples recorded in Acts chapters 2–5, when, from the Day of Pentecost, the Holy Spirit brought sweet unity, love and sharing among the believers.

BACKGROUND TO THE BOOK

It was out of a deep concern for love and unity in those churches which have experienced the renewing power of the Holy Spirit in recent years that two leadership consultations were called at Bawtry Hall in Yorkshire in January and March 1995. It was out of the papers given at those consultations and the subsequent discussion that this book has arisen. Its strength lies in the fact that all the writers are not only evangelical preachers of many years' experience but that they are each convinced of the presence, the power and the activity of the Holy Spirit in the church today, and that spiritual gifts may be exercised by all believers. All write, therefore, from within the charismatic movement, not as hostile observers from outside.

All the writers of this book have been involved in leadership in the charismatic movement from the early days. We write, not in the spirit of judgmentalism, or indeed with a negative critical attitude. Rather we write out of a deep concern for the church in which we have leadership responsibilities and for the future direction being taken by the charismatic movement. The prime purpose in writing is to draw attention to what we consider to be a serious drift away from biblically-based teaching into the realm of experientialism. This has led to the pernicious practice of using contemporary 'revelation' as the basis for doctrine and the justification for the formulation of new teaching and practice within the church which has no biblical foundation.

Each of the writers has undertaken in-depth research examining our own teaching and practice and a searching re-evaluation and re-assessment in the light of biblical scholarship. Our study of the Bible has led each of us to extend our personal re-evaluation to include current practices across the whole spectrum of the charismatic movement and to an examination in some detail of the underlying teaching. It is out of the fruit of this examination that this book has been written. It contains a message which we believe to be of vital importance in these days.

We recognise our own failings as leaders and our proneness to go astray in days when there are enormous pressures from the world around us and when we do not see very much to encourage us from the fruit of our labours. We therefore write in a spirit of love and humility under the deep conviction that the Bible provides us with the only standard of truth that can guard us against error, false doctrine, wrong practices and unrighteous behaviour.

DANGERS FACING THE CHURCH

It is our earnest hope that what we have written will be received by our brothers and sisters in Christ in the same spirit of love and humility in which we have written. Inevitably, in our examination of contemporary teaching in the charismatic movement we have to note those leaders who are most closely associated with its propagation. Our task, however, is not to make accusations against brothers in Christ, but rather to contend for the faith which we all hold to be precious and to warn where we see teaching which is seriously at variance with Scripture. Such teaching opens the door to all kinds of error and aberrant practices. There is grave danger today of the church being infiltrated by New Age teaching and the charismatic movement is not immune from this danger. Neither is it immune, if it drifts away from a strict adherence to the Bible as the plumb-line of divine revelation and truth, from straying into the realms of cultic activity.

Our warnings are sounded in days of great danger for the church. In the western industrialised nations we are faced with the continuing onslaught of secularism and rising hostility to the gospel in the context of increasing lawlessness and social decay. On the world scene Islamic fundamentalism and the use of violence to achieve their objectives is a continuing menace to the spread of the gospel and is resulting in many thousands of Christian martyrs each year.

David Barrett, editor of *The World Christian Encyclopedia*[2] estimates that there are currently over

300,000 Christians who lose their lives for the sake of the gospel each year. That number could soon be increased by martyrs in the post-Christian western nations as secularisation continues and opposition to the gospel grows.

Yet the worldwide church continues to grow through tremendous spiritual awakenings in many of the poorest non-industrialised nations. The greatest threat to their faith is the spread of westernisation and what we in the West have come to recognise as 'the pop culture' – the culture of easy affluence, sensuous self-indulgence, acquisitive materialism driven by moral and spiritual anarchy.

It is in the context of the contemporary world situation and our deep desire to see the re-evangelisation of the western nations, our own longings for revival and our unshakeable belief in the activity of the Holy Spirit among us in the church today that we have written this book. We call to our brothers and sisters in Christ to recognise the dangerous situation which faces us; and to recognise also that our emphasis upon the experiential within the charismatic movement has led us away from the doctrinal basis of the faith which our forefathers held to be of supreme importance. We therefore plead for a re-examination of current teaching and practice among charismatics in all branches of the church and a recognition that the Bible provides us with the only plumb-line of truth.

Our analysis required examining the teaching of a number of those who minister within the charismatic/evangelical churches. Inevitably in so doing we have had to name names. Our purpose is to compare what is being taught with what the Bible says. Our aim is not to discredit these men or to invalidate their ministries. Rather, it is our hope that what we have written will contribute to the ongoing theological debate within the charismatic movement.

Although this book is written against the background of the current debate on the Toronto Blessing, its scope is much wider. All the writers see Toronto as merely the latest step in a continuing process of an overemphasis upon experience and a neglect of sound biblical teaching. We have therefore attempted to look at the antecedents of Toronto rather than the phenomenon itself.

SYNOPSIS

What we have undertaken is essentially to re-trace our steps to the early days of the charismatic movement. We have looked at the introduction of different teachings, beliefs and practices at different stages in the development of the charismatic movement.

In Chapter Two I have undertaken a brief examination of the sociological background of the post-World War II period which has seen the rise of the charismatic movement. By examining the social history and secular culture of the age we can gain many helpful insights into the influences which mould our thinking and subtly allow the world to move into the church.

In Chapter Three Peter Fenwick looks back over his twenty-five years of leadership in the charismatic movement and re-assesses his own commitment to restorationist beliefs. This is an important contribution by an outstanding leader in the independent church sector. In Chapter Four David Forbes undertakes an examination of the Latter Rain Revival movement of the 1940s which had a considerable impact in North America, in both Canada and the USA. He notes the continuing influence of many of the teachings which emanated from that period and the effect they have had in the formation of charismatic doctrine.

In Chapter Five I have provided a review, with the help of David Forbes and some material supplied by Patricia Higton, of the outstanding prophecies which have come through the charismatic movement. I note two major types of prophecy, those giving forewarning of difficult times and those announcing times of blessing and revival. The chapter offers some assessment of the influence of contemporary prophecy on the growth and direction of the charismatic movement.

In Chapter Six David Noakes looks at the biblical basis of the charismatic movement and how it has developed over the past twenty-five or more years. He draws many penetrating insights from Scripture which illuminate the current church situation.

In the final chapter I have attempted to draw together the historical review undertaken in the book and to assess the way ahead.

When four writers tackle a subject, even though they each have specific tasks, inevitably there is some overlap. As editor I have tried to avoid repetition while exercising a minimum of editorial control. There are, however, one or two subjects which we have all examined such as the influence of the Kansas City prophets. We have each dealt with this from a different standpoint so that it is valid to hear each others' testimony as part of the historical review we have undertaken.

ACKNOWLEDGEMENTS

I would particularly like to acknowledge the help given by many church leaders whom I have consulted in the writing of this book. These have included a number of the early pioneers in the charismatic movement. I am particularly grateful to David Lillie, Beth Clark (widow of Denis Clark), Campbell McAlpine and Charles Pocock. I am also grateful to members of my own staff, Jean Wolton, Katherine Hallett and Andrew Lewis for their unstinting and efficient work in typing the manuscript and checking proofs. Finally, all the writers would like to express their gratitude to David Wavre of Eagle Publishers for his personal interest and the speed with which publication has been undertaken.

CHAPTER TWO

A CHILD OF THE AGE

'Ephraim mixes with the nations; . . . Foreigners sap his strength, but he does not realise it. His hair is sprinkled with grey, but he does not notice' (Hosea 7:8–9).

Since the days of the Industrial Revolution Britain has been a class-dominated society, the product of the twin forces of industrialisation and urbanisation, which broke the power of the landowners and the old social order of feudalism. This was replaced by the new social classes of entrepreneurs, industrialists, skilled craftsmen and unskilled workers. The latter formed a new class of landless peasants at the mercy of the owners of industry, who not only controlled the means of production but also owned the houses which their workers rented from them. Thus, from the earliest days of industrialisation, the British working classes saw themselves as the powerless ones who had to fight for survival against their economic oppressors. The seeds were sown of the class warfare which bedevilled British industry for two hundred years, the legacy of which is still with us today.

The beginning of the twentieth century saw the Labour movement beginning to become an organised political force, but it took two world wars in the first half of the century to break the social mould. The

Atlee government of 1945 was the first Socialist administration to obtain real power in Britain. Their legislative programme of social reform and reconstruction was to have far-reaching consequences which changed the face of Britain for the rest of the century.

The creation of the Welfare State with its boasted objective of caring for each individual from the cradle to the grave was designed to eliminate poverty and ensure justice for all. This objective was fully in line with the prevailing mood throughout the world which saw the post-war generation striving for freedom, justice, self-determination, equality and prosperity for all. In industrial societies this was expressed in various forms of socialism, while in non-industrial societies it was anti-colonialism and anti-imperialism. Marxism in various forms spread right across the world as an expression of the aspirations of the poor and oppressed. This was in harmony with the rise of black consciousness in societies dominated by whites and the rise of nationalism in countries dominated by foreign nationals or alien ethnic groups.

In retrospect the twentieth century may be seen as a period of the people versus the privileged; a revolution of the oppressed against the rulers and oppressors; a struggle for justice and freedom for all. By the middle of the century this movement reached a peak of political consciousness as it combined with the post-World War II period of reconstruction and the anti-war/pro-peace movement. During the 1950s and early 1960s the political expression of these aspirations reached its height with the achievement of independence in most of the former European colonial territories. In Asia, India, the Middle East, Africa, South America – the face of the world changed, the global map had to be redrawn.

During this same period a new movement was

birthed, particularly in the USA and Europe, an ideological and social movement destined to have as far-reaching effects as its political counterpart. It was what sociologists have termed 'the pop culture' – a spontaneous, youth-dominated ideological movement expressing the hopes and aspirations of the post-war generation in the rich industrial nations of the West. The prevailing economic and social conditions in these nations were ripe for just such an ideological movement. The post-war reconstruction period required massive building programmes of houses, offices, industrial plants and roads. The demand for labour was high which, in Britain, brought immigration from former colonies. But, even more significantly, it increased the wages of working people and opened up lifestyles beyond the imagination of former generations.

In Britain, for the first time in history, young people were able to command high wages. Even school leavers were able to go straight into unskilled work with large pay packets at the end of the week. Almost overnight a new consumer class was born with high purchasing power and with minimal social responsibilities. These were young single people with no families to support, no mortgages, but with money in their pockets. A free enterprise economy quickly adjusted to produce goods satisfying to the new consumer group. The market became youth-dominated in clothing fashions, records, hi-fi equipment, motorbikes, youth festivals, fast-food joints and a wide variety of material goods and activities designed to meet the desires and fulfil the demands of rapidly changing pop fashions

Public awareness of the birth of the new ideological movement dawned as a rude awakening. It came in 1956 with the arrival in Britain of an American film *Rock Around the Clock* featuring Bill Haley and a new strain of music known as 'rock 'n' roll'. The film was screened in a cinema at the Elephant and Castle, in south-east London. The largely teenage audience ripped up the seats and rocked in the aisles which sent shock waves through the nation. It was soon followed by a multitude of home-grown youth musicians, skiffle groups, guitarists and rock bands. The age of DIY had arrived. Young people did not simply want to be passive audiences, they wanted to do it themselves, either by being performers or at least joining actively in the physical activity of dancing, jiving, rocking and rolling, dressing up as Teddy boys or Mods and Rockers, driving in their motorcycle gangs and generally terrorising the older generation. The latter hailed the birth of the pop culture with a dread of the future, believing the whole world to have gone mad.

An important agent in creating the social conditions which gave rise to the pop culture was the education system which, during this period, experienced radical and far-reaching changes generated by a new educational philosophy. A new breed of teachers was produced in the post-war period, many of them with Marxist leanings, or at least strong socialist principles. They rejected the 'chalk and talk' Victorian methods of teaching which relied heavily on learning by rote. The new philosophy centred upon the 'discovery method' of education. Instead of an active teacher instructing a passive class of pupils, children were encouraged to discover facts for themselves. This meant that they no longer sat still and were punished for speaking; they were encouraged to work in groups, to carry out little research projects in the library, in the countryside or the city streets. Physical punishment was seen as degrading and offensive to the rights of children. This in turn had its effect upon family life and discipline in the home as well as social behaviour on the football terraces and in the city streets.

The ideological revolution which spawned the pop culture was aided, strengthened and, in many ways, made socially effective, by legislation. Many far-reaching social reforms were effected in a twenty-year period following World War II. It may be questioned whether they were responsible for the social revolution which has taken place in Britain in the second half of the twentieth century or whether they simply reflected the changing social values. It is probably a chicken and egg situation in which both are true as the one influenced the other.

The first major ideological reform was the repeal of the Witchcraft Act in 1957 and in the following year the Obscene Publications Act. These were followed in the 1960s by a string of measures effecting far-reaching social reform, dealing with race relations, capital punishment, homosexual acts, abortion and the discarding of censorship in publications and public entertainments. All these measures reflected the desire for freedom of choice and a society reputedly coming of age where people were able to make their own assessment of right and wrong, the good and the harmful.

The pop culture developed into a powerful social movement which created a society based upon 'situation ethics' rather than moral absolutes. In essence it was both hedonistic and individualistic. It was a society leaving behind the restrictions of the past and moving into new eras of individual freedom. Society was sailing into uncharted waters, driven by the strong winds of moral anarchy. Such a philosophy could only end in social anarchy – a society in which everyone does that which is right in their own eyes.

CHARACTERISTICS OF THE POP CULTURE

Youth dominated

The pop culture was essentially a youth culture which rejected the old, the outworn and the outdated. The emphasis was upon a search for new things and the discarding of the old. It was a culture from which, in the early days, the elderly felt shut out and devalued. Even in such things as clothing, the elderly felt disadvantaged as the consumer-driven market sought to satisfy the demands of the young.

The development of new technology in the brave new world emerging after the devastation of World War II reinforced the adulation of new things and led to the development of what was seen as 'the throw-away society'.

On the positive side, the period of reconstruction after the war needed the vitality and creativity of youth. It needed fresh energy, new ideas, unhindered by the failed policies of the past which had dragged the world into two devastating wars in the first half of the century. But the adoption of new ideas needed to be guided by firmly-rooted principles if confusion and chaos were to be avoided.

Anti-tradition

Any new movement contains an element of protest and rejection of the past. The pop culture was seeking to develop its own ideology and was therefore challenging traditional values. Inevitably the collected wisdom of the past was questioned as a whole new set of social mores applicable to the present day was sought.

Young people were quick to embrace the new ideas and to say that the policies pursued by their fathers had only led the world into the horrors of war culminating in the nuclear-bomb devastation of Hiroshima and Nagasaki. The anti-nuclear campaigns of CND linked with the more positive campaigns of the peace movement which produced the 'flower people' and slogans such as 'Make love not war'.

On the negative side, it increased awareness of racial differences and stirred passions. The campaign for racial justice had both a negative and positive side. Positively it affirmed the equality of all peoples regardless of race or colour while at the same time protesting against those traditions and institutions which debarred people on grounds of race, religion or ethnic origins.

The anti-traditionalism of the pop culture led to a despising of traditional institutions and even, in extreme cases, to the rejection of professionalism and scholarship. An extreme example was the Cultural Revolution in Communist China which persecuted and degraded teachers, university lecturers and scholars, often parading them through the streets as an act of public humiliation. In Britain there were not these extremes but public attitudes towards the professions changed radically. Teachers were no longer held in high esteem, neither were the clergy or any of those who served the public.

Individualism

The worldwide liberation movement of the post-war era spilled over into pop culture not only in politically-orientated protest movements but also in positive campaigns to alleviate suffering and to serve the world's poor and hungry. The 'Freedom from Hunger' campaign of the 1960s, the Oxford Campaign for Famine Relief which became Oxfam, and numerous others, all reflected the growing concern of the new generation for freedom, equality and justice. These social values were part of the growing recognition of the worth of each individual and the sanctity of human life. In emphasising these values the pop culture reacted against the wanton sacrifice of life in two world wars. It was also a reaction against what was seen as the oppression the ruling classes exercised over the world's poor and powerless peoples.

This recognition of the worth of each individual had its down side. What began as the pursuit of justice rapidly became a demand for rights. It was rights not privileges that changed attitudes towards the Welfare State in Britain. Instead of enjoying the privilege of living in a society where the needs of each individual were cared for by the whole community, these benefits were soon taken for granted. The younger generation knew nothing of the privations endured by former generations. Instead of thankfulness for the peace and security now enjoyed, the prevailing mood became a determination to obtain the maximum benefits available to each individual. Inner-city areas saw the rise of campaigns for community rights. 'Claimants Unions' sprang up in the 1970s to ensure that individuals were able to claim all their rights and entitlements from the State.

The campaigns for racial justice and justice for women soon produced minority group rights – feminist campaigns, the gay rights movement and the pro-abortion lobby with the campaign slogan 'A woman's right to choose'. These movements were fundamentally anti-social in that they contributed towards the breakdown of traditional family life and the downgrading of marriage. They were driven by a destructive spirit in which the only thing that mattered was the philosophy of individualism, in which personal morality and personal relationships are largely determined by the rights, desires and demands of the individual. The same determinants have played a creative role in the social values emerging from the pop culture. They are essentially anti-social and dysfunctional rather than creative of a healthy society. Their end product is the dissolution of society. The underlying lesson is that ethical nihilism leads to social nihilism. Moral anarchy leads to social anarchy.

Personal involvement

The post-war era of reconstruction that gave rise to the pop culture was an age of activity. The pop culture reflected this with all the dynamism of youth. They wanted to get involved personally in the radical changes that were already beginning to move from theory to practical reality by the beginning of the 1960s. The pop culture encouraged young people to get involved in their community, to take to the streets and demonstrate, to take their protests to the town hall or to turn the student union debate into days of action for better grants and living conditions.

The negative anti-professionalism of the pop culture also included a strong positive element of personal involvement in every kind of activity. It was the age of DIY. Do-it-yourself in home improvement resulted in an enormous industry of tools and provision for the amateur builder. DIY extended to every kind of activity from making your own music to arranging your own house conveyancing. DIY in education gave rise to the Open University, while DIY in sport and entertainment resulted in a boom in a wide variety of sporting activity, from athletics and field sports to aerobics and keep fit, to climbing and hang-gliding.

The pop culture initiated what was essentially the day of the amateur. Personal involvement plus lots of help from commercial products enabled the amateur to produce results every bit as good as the professional.

Sensuous

The pop culture rapidly swept away the old Victorian taboos on sex and the expression of emotions. It became a new age of freedom where the emphasis upon individual rights and personal involvement encouraged the exhibition rather than the suppression of the emotions. This was considered psychologically healthy. The Dr Spock generation of demand-fed babies and undisciplined children became the pop culture teenagers – the teeny-boppers who screamed wildly at their pop idols and lost themselves in waves of emotion at rock concerts and gigs. These activities paved the way for the drug-related rave parties of the 1990s.

The pop culture gave rise to a new age of sexual freedom aided by birth control and abortion. Sex education in schools followed the repeal of censorship in the entertainments industry allowing explicit sexual scenes on TV, film and video, as well as in books and magazines.

As the moral mores of the nations fell apart, so the media's reporting of scandals, details of violence and explicit sex became more lurid, both stimulating and feeding the appetite for the sensuous. Inevitably the intimate media accounts of the lifestyles of pop stars encouraged young people to follow the activities of their idols and imitate their behaviour.

Lawlessness

The radical change in the philosophy of education in the post-war era taught children not only to discover things for themselves but also to question traditional values, leading to the questioning of authority, social norms and religious beliefs. The latter was aided and abetted by the popularisation of liberal theology through books such as *Honest to God* by John Robinson, the bishop who had defended the publication of *Lady Chatterley's Lover*, which broke new ground in explicitly sexual literature.

The old norms, moral precepts and social values, together with their foundational religious beliefs rooted in the Judeo-Christian faith, were rapidly crumbling. By the middle of the 1960s the pop culture had become an unstoppable bandwaggon rolling the nation into a social revolution the end product of which only the exceptionally far-sighted could see.

The breakdown of moral absolutes left the field wide open for 'situation ethics' in which the rights and wrongs of every action for each individual would have to be sought within the prevailing situation and circumstances. This paved the way for increasing lawlessness, for the lowering of standards of professional conduct, and for radical changes in business ethics and the practices of corporate institutions. Thus the way was open for corruption in politics, industry and commerce leading inevitably to the increase of crime, drugs, family breakdown, child abuse, street violence and terrorism.

The pop culture was a child of revolt. It was born out of a spirit of rebellion – essentially a destructive rather than a creative spirit. Its anti-traditionalism was essentially the rejection of morality, of fundamental belief and of law. It was DIY in the rules of behaviour with a self-centred individualism that was essentially destructive of community. It was social anarchy and the inevitable result of anarchy is the destruction of society.

Power

We live in an age of powerlessness. Two world wars in the first half of the century swept millions of men and women from many nations into the horror of modern armed conflict. They had no option but to fight and even those who remained at home were mercilessly bombed in cities throughout Europe and were powerless to defend themselves.

The post-war period of reconstruction saw thousands of inner-city communities destroyed as their homes were bulldozed and replaced by tower blocks. Others saw their homes destroyed to make way for motorways which they were powerless to resist.

As radical social changes were enforced by law, foundational social values began to crumble, moral principles were neglected, marriage breakdown increased, the stability of family life was undermined, crime rates soared and a general sense of powerlessness to withstand the onslaught of the forces of social change became widespread. The genie was out of the bottle and no one had the power to put it back.

The economic boom years gave way to recession. Powerful commercial enterprises collapsed, bankruptcies increased, mortgage lenders foreclosed on the homes of defaulting houseowners. The Englishman's castle was built on sand. People were powerless even to defend their homes.

The sense of powerlessness was increased by Europeanisation. Europe was swallowing up the little island which had fiercely maintained its freedom and independence against all invaders for a thousand years. Norman Tebitt summed it up when he said that the day would come when the 'Chancellor's budget speech would be faxed from Frankfurt'. The politicians, the government, the cabinet and the Prime Minister all share the sense of powerlessness to withstand the forces of change which are sweeping across the nation. Even the Queen had her 'annus horribilis', being powerless to defend her family from the adulterous and rebellious spirits of the age.

THE CHARISMATIC MOVEMENT

In the midst of these traumatic social changes and upheaval a new phenomenon appeared within the church: the charismatic movement, which did not however arise in the immediate post-World War II period. In fact it had no clear beginnings. There was no mighty outpouring of the Spirit of God as on the Day of Pentecost, no fresh outpouring of the Holy Spirit as at the beginning of the Pentecostal movement at Azusa Street in 1906; there was no great revival, no clear move of God resulting in the conversion of multitudes of unbelievers.

Most charismatic leaders today trace the beginnings of the movement to the middle or late 1960s. But the first really recognisable signs of a movement did not occur until the early 1970s, when home-based fellowships or 'house-churches' began to proliferate.

Whatever date we assign to the beginnings of the charismatic movement, it has to be acknowledged that the pop culture was already a firmly established part of the social scene. The destructive effects of the spirit of rebellion could be clearly seen, biblical belief was under attack, traditional morality was in rapid decline, so too was church attendance. The church, especially in inner-city areas, was in the full flight of retreat with a high closure rate of redundant church buildings, especially in areas of immigrant settlement. It was against the background of spiritual atrophy and moribund institutionalism in the mainline churches that the charismatic movement emerged. It was born out of the womb of frustration with the *status quo* rather than through a notable move of the Spirit of God.

The charismatic movement came to birth at a time when the spirit of moral and social rebellion was triumphing in the battle with traditionalism in the secular world. This was the time when the most socially destructive Acts of Parliament were put on the Statute Book. It was a time when it seemed as though the whole nation was intent upon overturning past tradition and rejecting the social values and moral precepts of their forefathers. This was the spirit of the age in which the charismatic movement emerged and there is good evidence for the contention that many of the social characteristics of that period were birthed into it, the significance of which we are only now beginning to see.

We may go farther and ask the question, 'Was the charismatic movement a move of God? Was it actually initiated by the Lord Jesus, the Head of the church?' It is not easy to give an unequivocable affirmative to that question due to its lack of a clear beginning and the fact that it was not rooted in the conviction of sin, repentance and revival. There was not even a great wave of renewal sweeping through the church or a 'holiness' movement characterised by self-denial, humility, self-sacrificial suffering with the major emphasis upon the cross. These are the characteristics of the present-day church in China which has arisen out of the flames of persecution and martyrdom of the saints. In China there was no spectacular outpouring of the Spirit in any one place to mark the beginning of the period of great spiritual awakening now seeping through that nation, but there were all the marks of authentic New Testament spirituality including a willingness to die for the faith.

The charismatic movement, by contrast, had none of these marks and it is for this reason that we may fairly ask whether it, 'was the creation of God or man'? In fact, it bore many of the social characteristics of the western nations in which it arose. It developed in an environment of easy affluence and it offered a form of spirituality which appealed strongly to the rising new middle-classes seeking quick self-advancement and status in the new post-war social order. Before offering an answer to the question of origins we will look at the characteristics of the charismatic movement under the same headings as we used when looking at the pop culture.

Youth dominated

Many of the founding fathers of the charismatic movement in Britain were men of deep spirituality, personal commitment to the Lord Jesus and with a passion to share Christ with others. Many of them, such as Denis Clark, Arthur Wallis, David Lillie, Campbell McAlpine, Michael Harper and Tom Smail to mention just a few, were steeped in the Word of God and utterly committed to the promotion of New Testament Christianity. This, indeed, was their major objective, namely the restoration of authentic New Testament principles to the life of the church. David Lilley has held on to this vision for more than forty years. It is a vision for what he calls 'a God-centred perspective' which he believes should 'characterise the communal life of every normal New Testament church'.[1]

There were many other men from conservative evangelical or Brethren backgrounds whose study of the Word of God led them to believe that the twentieth-century church had strayed woefully from the New Testament pattern. They longed to see the restoration of the fivefold ministries, of the recognition of baptism in the Holy Spirit and of the exercise of spiritual gifts within the church. Their witness within their denominational institutions often stirred heated opposition and many were ejected from their fellowships.

In the late 1960s and early 1970s a few house-church groups began to be formed, although this was never the intention of those who longed to see the restoration of New Testament teaching and practice in the church. In the early days there were men in leadership of these new fellowships who were of sound biblical scholarship and considerable spiritual maturity. But, as so often happens in a new movement, it is not the thinkers who prevail but those who are the most convincing 'charismatic' personalities, popular speakers and natural leaders. Young men rapidly took the initiative, both in forming new fellowships and in taking leadership. This was fully in line with the prevailing mood in western society. These young men owed no allegiance to traditional church or denominational institutions. They were untrained for leadership and most of them had no theological education. They rapidly developed new styles of worship using guitars, which were ideal for home-groups, and new styles of meetings and leadership.

Anti-tradition

The new house-fellowships soon attracted those who were discontented with their traditional denominational churches. This, of course, is inevitable with any new movement. When David was outlawed by King Saul and took refuge in the hills it is recorded that, 'All those who were in distress or in debt or discontented gathered round him, and he became their leader' (1 Sam 22:2).

Something like this happened in the early days of the house-church movement. Many who were dissatisfied with the lifelessness of the denominational churches were attracted by the informality and freshness of the house-church fellowships. The early days saw many groups split away from a parent group and form new fellowships. These splits often occurred on the grounds of teaching or practice, but in reality new young leaders were arising to challenge an established leader and form their own fellowships.

The emphasis was upon all things new in response to the new experience of the baptism in the Holy Spirit. This was a new day. God was doing a new thing. Old established practices in the denominational churches were considered stumbling-blocks to what God wanted to do among his people. The Holy Spirit was sweeping away the dead wood in the church and there were many calls for people to come out of the mainline churches because God had finished with the denominations.

These calls did not come from mature Bible teachers such as Denis Clark and Campbell McAlpine who never formed new fellowships and whose ministries were transdenominational. They came from the young men who eagerly seized the opportunities for leadership presented by the new teaching and the impatience of many within the traditional churches to move faster than their pastors deemed to be wise. In Brighton, for example, when Terry Virgo founded the Clarendon Fellowship he was joined by a large proportion of the congregation from St Luke's, Brighton and Hangelton Baptist as well as individual members from churches in the surrounding area.

Similar things happened in many other parts of the country where house-fellowships sprang up and rapidly attracted members of the mainline churches who were longing to experience new life in the Spirit and who felt constricted by the traditions which bound them in the churches they had attended for many years. It was a time of splits, of fission and fusion, as house-fellowships multiplied, outgrew their drawing-room bases and began worshipping in scout huts and school halls. There were many cries of sheep stealing and counter charges of being blocks to the Holy Spirit. There were many hurts, but it is now a long time ago and most wounds have healed – the new fellowships are an established part of the church scene. Their leaders are prominent in the charismatic movement alongside those in the mainline churches.

Most of the new fellowships planted in the 1970s or early 1980s have now aligned themselves with one or other of half a dozen streams such as Pioneer, New Frontiers, New Covenant or Ichthus, each of which is now an independent sect or a mini-denomination. At the time these new fellowships were being formed a significant renewal movement was taking place within the main-line churches themselves. Many ordained ministers quite independently experienced the baptism of the Holy Spirit and began to lead their congregations into renewal in the Holy Spirit. Many suffered considerably in doing so while others saw quite spectacular results. Colin Urquhart in Luton, Trevor Dearing in Hainault, David Watson in York, David Pawson in Guildford and many others, each attracted large congregations and saw the renewing of the spiritual life in the churches they led and the exercise of spiritual gifts among the people.

It is questionable in hindsight whether it was ever right to fragment the church by the formation of numerous new fellowships or whether it was God's intention to renew the existing structures. The new eager young leaders reflected the spirit of the age both in their impatience to get on with the new thing and with their anti-traditionalism which regarded all things of the past as only being fit for ridicule and rejection. Certainly the church was in need of a radical shake up and spiritual renewal; but was it really necessary to tear apart the Body of Christ so wantonly and create such division? Would a little more love and patience have enabled renewal and a new unity to run right across the denominations? Was this God's intention for his church?

We shall never know the answers to these questions but it is a fact that the decade of the 1970s which saw the greatest fragmentation of the church was the decade of the greatest social unrest, the height of the social revolution. The spirit of rebellion was running right through the nation with numerous strikes in industry, a vast increase in marriage breakdown and sexual promiscuity with all the accompanying evidence of the rejection of tradition and the eager pursuit of new social and moral values. It is perhaps a strange quirk that the young rebel leaders who caused great division in the 1970s and who are now the leading 'apostles' of the charismatic movement are the very ones calling for unity and condemning as 'divisive' those who question the biblical validity of their teaching and practices.

Individualism

Twentieth-century evangelicalism has tended towards individualism due to its emphasis upon the personal nature of salvation. The seeds of individualism have been there since the Reformation but twentieth-century western culture has greatly encouraged this. By the time the charismatic movement was born, individualism in western society was rampant and the new renewal movement embraced it wholeheartedly.

Unlike the corporate experience of the disciples on the Day of Pentecost the renewal movement is entirely personal. Its emphasis is upon the personal relationship of each believer with the Father. This, of course, is perfectly biblical and in line with the promise of the Lord, but the Hebraic background to Jesus' teaching has been lost over the centuries and with it the understanding of the place of each believer within the corporate community – the Body of Christ. Charismatic renewal is highly 'me-centred'. Each individual is encouraged to discover their spiritual gifting. Indeed, the gifts are regarded as personal possessions rather than together making up the spiritual attributes of the community of believers.

This individualistic concept of the gifts has led to some erroneous teaching, highly dangerous for the health of the church, such as the 'positive confession' or 'faith movement' which has emphasised physical and materialistic values such as health and wealth. Its proponents have taught that God wants all his people to prosper, to be healthy and wealthy and that through faith or 'positive confession' these things can be obtained. This teaching is fully in line with the desires and ambitions of western acquisitive materialistic society which no doubt accounts for its popularity among charismatics despite it being the very opposite of the teaching of Jesus!

Much of the preoccupation of charismatics with the exercise of spiritual gifts has been me-centred – me and my health, my wealth, my family and my personal relationship with God. The exercise of spiritual gifts thereby tends to meet the personal needs within the fellowship. The servant nature of discipleship – saved to serve – tends to become lost.

Charismatic worship has both reflected this me-centredness and helped to reinforce it. A very large number of worship songs and choruses use the first person singular rather than plural. One of the great benefits of the renewal movement has been to heighten each believer's awareness of the presence of God and thereby to heighten each individual's active participation in worship and deepen their spiritual apprehension of God. This is wholly good, but the danger of an overemphasis on individualism is a loss of the corporate and thereby a loss of the essential nature of the New Testament church as the Body of Christ.

Personal involvement

If you walk into a strange church you can usually know instantly whether it is charismatic or traditional. If it is traditional the congregation will fill up the back pews first; if it is charismatic they will fill up from the front. In the traditional church the congregation is passive, the people are there to be ministered to by choir, readers and preacher; in the charismatic church the people are there for active participation. They want to be fully involved in worship with the freedom to wave their arms, clap, dance and give physical expression to their emotions.

This DIY worship is very much in line with the spirit of the pop culture. Amateur musicians, worship leaders and singers give a performance at the front which is enthusiastically supplemented by the active participation of the congregation. In the new sects which have arisen out of the house-church fellowships the preachers and pastors are also untrained. Hardly any of them have had any formal theological training in a theological college or university theology faculty. A few have been to a Bible School although many of the younger leaders have received some sort of training from schools set up within their own sects. These are non-academic and simply pass on the limited teaching of the leadership. This represents one of the greatest dangers of the charismatic movement where the emphasis has been increasingly experience-centred or revelationary with increasingly less emphasis upon biblical scholarship.

As the charismatic movement has tended to become increasingly driven by the leaders of the new sects in concert with a handful of leaders from the mainline churches, few of whom are men of outstanding scholarship, the gap between biblical truth and current charismatic practice has widened. The anti-professionalism of the pop culture has been present in the charismatic movement from the beginning although leaders have been quick to assert their own authority. The excesses of heavy shepherding, which scarred many people's lives during the 1980s have largely disappeared, although the authoritarianism of sectarian leadership has left its mark. Individual believers are encouraged to be fully involved in worship and the exercise of spiritual gifts with the exception of the gift of prophecy. This is permitted as long as it is supportive of the leadership.

Sensuous

The charismatic movement has encouraged the physical expression of emotion. The new songs, new forms of worship and freedom of expression have been a wonderfully liberating experience for millions of believers who have felt repressed and oppressed within the institutionalised traditions of the mainline churches. The renewal movement has come like a breath of fresh air in a stale room. It has brought new life and vitality not only to worship but also to evangelism and outreach into the community in many churches. The experience of being filled with the Spirit is a transforming and life-giving event which no one who has entered into it would ever wish to deny.

Yet this same liberating experience has had dangerous side effects. The new liberty and freedom enjoyed by charismatics in their worship has extended into personal relationships where Spirit-filled believers are regarded as a specially-favoured group, honoured by God and thereby standing in a special relationship not only to him but to each other. The emphasis upon freedom and informality is accompanied by biblical teaching giving an emphasis upon 'grace' rather than 'law' which has tended to create an atmosphere of permissiveness in personal relationships.

There have been many casualties of this charismatic freedom such as the church in South Wales in the early 1980s where a 'prophecy' was received that every one should have a spiritual partner. They set about fulfilling this 'prophecy' regardless of sex or marriage relationships. Close partnerships often excluded a spouse and spiritual intimacy soon included physical intimacy. Even the pastor was caught up in this and had to come to repentance and renounce the policy before the whole church moved into disaster.

Other problems have occurred through practices associated with deliverance from demonic possession. This has included a teaching that demons need to be exorcised from their point of entry into the body. Those who have been victims of sexual abuse have been ministered to by the laying on of hands and anointing with oil in their private parts. There are indications that these practices are much more widespread than the few highly-publicised reports.

The very widespread publicity given to the 'Nine-O'Clock Service' – a Sheffield-based charismatic rave-type worship led by the Reverend Chris Brain shocked the nation in August 1995. The NOS was originally based at St Thomas' Crookes Parish Church under Robert Warren but complaints from neighbours about the noise led to its breakaway and independent operation under the unsupervised leadership of Chris Brain.

He used hard rock music, strobe lights and wild dancing by scantily-clad girls in his rave-type trendy services aimed to attract young people raised in the pop culture. The NOS aimed to make them feel at home and comfortable with the Gospel presentation.

Stephen Lowe, Archdeacon of Sheffield was

reported in the press to have said that about twenty women had allegedly been sexually abused by Brain who practised intimate laying on of hands for healing and deliverance. Press reports linked Chris Brain with John Wimber from whom he was said to have learned his healing practices. Wimber was reported in the press as saying, 'We encouraged Chris's church and gave a gift to enable the Nine-O'Clock Service to get started'.[2] Brain not only had links with Wimber but was also strongly attracted to Matthew Fox's New Age teachings. The lurid press reports indicated that the NOS was moving dangerously close to the inclusion of sexual practices as part of worship.

A major weakness of the charismatic movement is that its teaching has not had a strong emphasis upon moral values. Its anti-legalism has in fact left the door open to worldly standards of sexual freedom to become commonplace. Charismatic churches throughout Britain have suffered from adulterous relationships and marriage breakdown. This has been common, not only in the house-church streams, but also in the main-line charismatic churches. There are no comparative figures available, but from personal knowledge of the church scene across the denominations I would estimate that the incidence of adultery and marriage breakdown among leaders and church members in the charismatic churches is considerably greater than in non-charismatic churches. This is further evidence of the influence of the world and especially the pop culture.

Lawlessness

An untrained leadership in the new independent churches has given itself great freedom to develop along lines untrammelled by the kind of ministerial and clergy professionalism of leaders in the mainline churches. From the earliest days there has been difficulty over accountability. House-churches were often led by a single leader who assumed autonomous control. Other fellowships developed team leaderships or elderships with shared authority. Even these could be highly authoritarian and were not accountable to church members' meetings as in the mainline churches.

More recently there has been a coming together of most independent fellowships into 'streams' or sects each with their own form of hierarchical authority. In some of these the top leader is recognised as an 'apostle' and the apostles of the different streams sometimes recognise a form of accountability to each other on a network basis.

Authority within the charismatic movement is a problem. The Pentecostal movement at the beginning of the century rapidly developed structures of organisation and accountability but the charismatic movement has produced no such equivalent. This is, no doubt, partly because the renewal has run right across denominational lines from Roman Catholic to Brethren. This lack of authority structure within the movement is also partly accounted for by the social environment in which it was born. The 1960s and 1970s were years of radical social change when all established mores and past traditions were being challenged. It was essentially a period of social anarchy which was birthed into the charismatic movement. It was a spirit that resisted traditional authority, yet its leaders often insisted upon a greater obedience to them by their church members than is accorded to ministers in the mainline churches from which they broke away to seek a new freedom!

Attitudes to authority within the charismatic movement have tended to adulate leaders, especially those with high-profile ministries. This has had a serious detrimental effect upon the exercise of discernment by individual church members. The teaching of the leader is regarded as sacrosanct. Individual members are not encouraged to challenge their teaching or practices, which leaves the people wide open to deception if the leaders themselves go astray.

This teaching prepared the way for the rapid spread of the Toronto phenomenon initiated by Rodney Howard-Browne who spent some years prior to Toronto working on his method of transmitting what he calls his 'ministry of laughter'. Speaking to a meeting in Birmingham in June 1994 he exhorted people to submit their wills to him and not to weigh what was happening. 'Don't try to work it out with your natural mind,' he said, 'for the things of the Spirit of God are foolishness to the natural mind.' His hypnotic technique soon had the whole audience under his control falling about in uncontrollable laughter and physical jerks. Clearly none of them realised they were being duped with false teaching because if they are born-again believers they do not have a 'natural mind'. The mind of the believer is renewed by the Spirit of God (Rom 12:2) which also enables us to know the truth and to resist deception provided we do not submit ourselves to charlatans and deceivers!

Power

John Wimber came to Britain in the 1980s to a nation steeped in a sense of powerlessness from loss of empire and world prestige. The church was suffering from forty years of steep decline which leaders were powerless to stem. Wimber came with a promise of power – divine power, Holy Spirit power – available to all Spirit-filled believers if they would allow themselves to be released from the shackles of tradition and let the Holy Spirit flow through them.

This message could not have been more apt. Power

to the powerless. It was exactly what British Christians wanted. Leaders and people lapped it up. No more doom and gloom. No more struggling against uneven odds. Here was real power to give victory – to triumph over the powers of darkness. The devil had had the church on the run for far too long, here at last was the power to overcome the enemy. Wimber taught that all adversity, including ill health, could be due to demonic activity. Through the power of the Holy Spirit, sickness could be overcome and even cancer healed. An even more popular promise was that ordinary believers could exercise the gift of healing provided they learned the techniques and had the faith. They could drive out demons and scatter the enemies of the gospel.

Wimber also brought a new concept of evangelism, coining the term 'power evangelism'. This was just what charismatics wanted to hear. They were able to discard the old-fashioned gospel presentations of Billy Graham and crusade evangelism with its calls for repentance. Here was something new and exciting. They only had to believe and the Holy Spirit would do it through signs and wonders which would astonish the unbelievers and bring them flocking into the Kingdom. It was a 'Kingdom Now' theology that appealed strongly to a generation raised on instant results – instant food, instant credit, instant news.

In 1990 Wimber came back with the Kansas City 'prophets', having embraced their Latter Rain teachings of a great end-time harvest to be reaped by an irresistible 'Joel's army' of overcomers, which fitted neatly into Wimber's concept of power evangelism – they even promised power to overcome the final enemy, death, and enable the elite company of the elect to be part of the final generation, the immortal Bride of Christ.

Four years later, just as the backlash of unfulfilled

promises and false prophecy was plunging charismatic churches into gloom and the new churches had plateaued, the Toronto Blessing burst upon the scene with its new wave of promises of power – power in the most attractive form of all – power for self.

This came at a time of great vulnerability for British charismatics. Many leaders confessed to being spiritually dry, discouraged and disappointed. The great wave of prophecy had come to nothing. Promises to leaders that they would be preaching to multitudes in sports stadia and arenas and witnessing before princes and powerful leaders, all now had a hollow ring. Their leadership was on the line. They threw themselves into some highly-publicised outreaches with expansive promises – the JIM campaign which was supposed to produce 5 million converts went off like a damp squib. So too did the Revival Fire campaign. Reinhardt Bonnke's much publicised and highly expensive £7 million campaign raised even higher expectations but proved to be the most spectacular failure of them all with a mere 16,000 responses from a mail drop to 24 million households.

British charismatic and Pentecostal leaders were at an all time low at the very moment when they heard that something new was happening across the Atlantic. A new fountain of spiritual life was flowing in Toronto promising a new filling of divine power. It was wonderful news to know that God was giving revival somewhere in the western world where for twenty years we had only heard of news of great awakenings among the poor non-industrial nations where church congregations were numbered in their thousands or tens of thousands. But the most exciting news was that the blessing was transportable! Eleanor Mumford (wife of the leader of the South London Vineyard Fellowship), had been and got it, and brought it back, and passed it on to others. If she could do it surely others could do the same. Here was real hope for hard-pressed pastors struggling to maintain their local church witness – they rushed to book their flights to Toronto. Very few went to test the spirits in obedience to New Testament teaching. They were more interested in the simple pragmatic test – Does it work? Will it work for me? They reached out eager hands to any from the hastily-enlisted local leadership team who had got 'it' and would pass 'it' on to them. They fell about laughing, twitching and roaring, then hurried back to pass 'it' onto others.

The latest power trip had arrived!

The child of the age – the age of powerlessness – had reached adolescence. As John Arnott, pastor of the Toronto Vineyard Church, put it 'It's party time! We are like little children coming to their father to play.'

CONCLUSION

After twenty-five years of the charismatic renewal movement all we have to show for it in Britain is a nation infinitely worse in its moral, spiritual and social behaviour – a nation facing economic collapse and social disaster – while many of those to whom God has entrusted the precious gifts of his Holy Spirit fall about in uncontrollable laughter. There are many indications that we are near to the point when the world's economy will crumble and a period of unprecedented lawlessness will sweep across the nations.

If ever the church were needed to take up the mantle of the prophet to declare the Word of the Living God and the way of salvation as the only hope for mankind it is surely today! The charismatic/evangelical sector of the church believes the Bible to be the Word of God and also acknowledges the presence and power of the Holy Spirit among his people. But today these very churches are being torn asunder by division resulting from the excitement of fleshy manifestations which are a massive diversion and distraction preventing the church from fulfilling the real purposes of God.

The Holy Spirit has indeed been poured out in abundance throughout this century. The Spirit of God does indeed give us supernatural power, but it is not power for self-aggrandisement or power for self-fulfilment, or power to exercise power over other sinners, but power to declare the Word of the Living God with power and authority. When will we stop playing the world's games? When will we come to our senses like the prodigal son and return to the Father? Will the charismatic movement have to come to total disaster before we realise how grossly we have been deceived and how we have prostituted the precious gifts of the Holy Spirit and sold our birthright for a mess of pottage?

What is the answer to the question, 'Was the charismatic movement initiated by God?' We shall delay attempting an answer to the last chapter, when we will have considered other aspects of the history and development of the movement.

CHAPTER THREE

THE ROOTS OF THE TORONTO BLESSING

It is the church's task to proclaim God's will and intentions to the world – a world which over the past fifty years has progressively abandoned God's laws and standards. The condition of society is now so serious that many Christians, myself included, believe that only a full-scale revival can reverse this moral decline. Since January 1994 the Toronto Blessing has been hailed as either a great revival or its precursor. Because of the earnest desire for revival in the hearts of many it is understandable that these claims have been widely accepted, but we must recognise that their hopes and expectations have led many people to embrace the movement without fully considering all the implications. Can we be sure that the Toronto Blessing is a genuine move of God? There are many features of the Toronto Blessing which give me grave cause for concern; features which, if unchecked, will seriously impair the church's ability to perform its God-given task.

My greatest fear springs from the fact that the Bible no longer occupies the place which once it did in the evangelical community. Indeed the whole controversy surrounding the Toronto Blessing is in fact a major battle for the Bible. Traditionally, evangelicals have sought a firm biblical foundation for all matters relating to doctrine and conduct. It is my contention that the Toronto Blessing represents the most recent stage in a process whereby this tradition is being gradually eroded. Am I right to fear that it will soon be abandoned altogether?

In this chapter I will set out the stages which preceded the Toronto Blessing in the process of erosion to which I have referred. It will, I hope, become clear that the Toronto Blessing is no sudden or unexpected phenomenon; but that in fact the ground has been well prepared by the acceptance of previous unbiblical practices. I will also offer an explanation as to why the church has become vulnerable to such errors. Finally, I will indicate the features of the Toronto Blessing which are unbiblical.

UNBIBLICAL PRACTICES

During the last fifteen years a number of practices have been introduced, mostly in the charismatic churches, which have either no biblical foundation or only a very dubious one. These practices have been accepted without question and are now a normal part of much charismatic theology. Here are some examples.

End of meetings ministry times

This is now a normal part of many charismatic meetings both in churches and in joint celebrations. People are called forward for prayer and usually laying on of hands with a view to deliverance from rejections, hurts, abuses, fears, inadequacies and such-like; the hope is that they will go on in a more positive way of living. Sometimes people are prayed for in order to receive particular gifts. Usually the subjects of prayer have little, if anything, to do with the content of the sermon.

All of this has been a common part of charismatic meetings for a long time, despite the fact that there is neither precedent nor teaching anywhere in the New Testament for this practice. It has to be said that it has not created any significant opposition, since it has seemed harmless enough and has surely been practised out of good motives; what can possibly be wrong with seeking to bless someone? The fact that in many cases the same people come forward time after time has also not raised too many questions.

The 'Word of Knowledge' healing meetings

This again is a very common charismatic practice. Someone, usually from the front of the church, but not exclusively so, makes a succession of statements to the effect that, 'There is someone here with . . .' and there follows the recital of a number of ailments. People are expected to stand, declaring themselves to be the person referred to. Prayer is made and the whole procedure moves on. There is often little or no checking out as to whether a healing has taken place. However, the real point at issue is that this technique was never practised by Jesus nor by any of the apostles at any point in the whole of the New Testament. This has not been considered important by those concerned, since the assumption is that from time to time some people do actually get healed, and therefore the feeling is that if it works, albeit occasionally, it is acceptable.

Demons as the cause of sin

Over the last twenty years there has been an ever-increasing tendency to identify demons as a primary cause of sin in Christians. It goes without saying that, if a demon is causing certain sinful human behaviour, then repentance for sins is not appropriate, and is rarely called for; the matter will be dealt with by exorcism. The blame for sin can be laid fully at the door of the demon. Once again this is profoundly contrary to New Testament practice and teaching.

The doctrine of territorial spirits

It has for a number of years been sweepingly assumed that hamlets, towns, cities or nations are dominated by specific spirits whose size and power is appropriate to the population mass over which they are said to rule. It is consequently assumed that effective evangelisation of such a location will not happen until these territorial spirits have been engaged in spiritual warfare and decisively expelled. This is not the same as praying for the conversion of one's friends and family. It is praying for the extermination of these evil spirits and very often actually addressing them.

There is not a shred of New Testament teaching or practice to support this kind of activity, and the theology of it is based on a passage in Daniel 10:13 where the Prince of the kingdom of Persia is said to have withstood an angelic helper sent by God to Daniel. This Prince of the kingdom of Persia hindered the angel for twenty-one days. It is pure speculation to assert that this Prince was a demon. Since Daniel was not waging spiritual warfare in the modern sense of the word; since there is not another single example in the whole of the Bible of this sort of activity; and since we are given no theological explanation of it all, it is therefore astonishing that a definitive theology has been built up from this brief incident and has introduced into the charismatic church what is now a very dominant practice. As I have already said, this practice is deemed to be vitally necessary before proper evangelisation of a particular territory can be expected to succeed. For almost two-thousand years the church has not known this dogma and consequently has been unable to engage in this activity. It is amazing that it has nevertheless achieved such astounding success at different times and in different places.

CHRISTIANS VULNERABLE TO ERROR

The whole point of presenting these examples (and there are others) is to demonstrate that the charismatic movement has been taking on board teaching and practices that have either no, or at best flimsy, biblical foundation and turning them into dogma. It is almost certainly true that many members of charismatic churches do believe that there actually is a biblical foundation, and this fact will raise a different concern later in this chapter. But the ground for accepting such practices has been well and truly prepared and into this situation there has come an even more unbiblical teaching, namely the Toronto Blessing.

We turn now to two factors which have made the charismatic church most vulnerable to departures from biblical truth and practice.

Restorationism

In the 1970s most of the new churches, as the house churches are now called, were swept by Restorationist teaching which created great expectations of triumph for the church of God. It was embraced as a very welcome antidote to the widespread and gloomy views of the church's future which had been disseminated by Dispensationalist teaching. According to that Dispensationalist view the church on earth could look forward only to deterioration leading to failure and ignominy. As is so often the case, one extreme position was rejected, only for another to be embraced.

Restorationism came presenting an absolutely opposite view of the church, and taught that the church would in this age, and before the return of Jesus, become overwhelmingly successful in every area of human life. In particular this meant that the church would overwhelm the secular world, not by military means, but by the force of righteousness. The church's influence would be so massive and extensive that it would dominate government, education, business and finance, the judiciary, law enforcement, the arts etc. This did not mean that there would necessarily be a Christian political party in Parliament; that would not be necessary. The church would be seen to be so glorious in wisdom and righteousness that government and political leaders everywhere would come to it for counsel and advice. Education planners and captains of industry as well as leaders in other fields of human activity would all in similar fashion be accepting the church's standards and the church's direction for their affairs. The righteous rule of Christ which is foretold following the return of Christ to the earth would be in very large measure realised before his return.

Almost as a by-product, the church and its members would become wealthy as a grateful world brought its riches and laid them at the church's feet. Such beliefs clearly opened the door wide for the health and wealth errors of the so-called 'Faith Movement'.

It was strongly felt that evangelism would probably not be needed. It would be enough for non-Christians to see how good the 'new brand' of Christianity was as relationships were put right, and as Christians loved and served each other and bore each other's burdens.

They would voluntarily press into the church in great numbers and thus be readily converted. Persecution was not really expected, failure was out of the question, and trials and tribulations were not on anyone's agenda.

It must be said that the errors of Restorationism, and errors they are, did not result from the Bible being by-passed as I have earlier described concerning other practices. On the contrary, extensive appeal was made to the Bible. It is not within the scope of this chapter to thoroughly examine what went wrong. But the nub of the error was as follows.

Jesus and the apostles, as recorded in the New Testament, took many statements and incidents from the Old Testament and applied them to the church, thus usually giving them a wider meaning. These statements and incidents originally concerned either certain individuals or the whole Jewish people. Restorationist teaching followed that pattern and applied it to other Old Testament passages and transferred them to the church. I submit to the reader that this approach is not legitimate. Jesus was the divine Son of God and knew all things. He therefore had an absolute right to say which Old Testament passages apply to the church and which do not. Furthermore, to the apostles was given the Spirit of Truth in order to lead them into all truth. We believe the results of this have been vouchsafed to us for all time in the New Testament. We may trust that Jesus and the apostles have drawn to our attention all those passages of the Old Testament which can be applied to the church.

Without doubt Restorationism was an ultimate statement of over-realised eschatology. What is more, its expectations were to happen soon. When this was being declared in the 1970s and the early 1980s, no one seriously believed that the year 2000 might arrive without much of this victory already well in place. The expectations amongst the people of God were quite enormous and they would return in their thousands from the great Bible weeks fully expecting to see progress within the following months. Naturally the churches themselves expected to see a power and beauty which far exceeded anything that had been experienced in the previous two thousand years of church history. Attempts were made to show that throughout the years, certainly since the Reformation, the church had become, by successive stages, more powerful and more beautiful, and now the ultimate was about to be achieved. It must be said that there was a great deal of human pride in all of this. It was believed that it would be the charismatic churches which would achieve this, and in particular, the Restorationist charismatic churches. They would pave the way for the other churches to participate, provided of course those other churches embraced Restorationist principles. If they did not, they would be completely by-passed by God himself as he fulfilled his purposes in the earth.

None of this has happened. None of these massive expectations have been fulfilled and many of the people who were in receipt of those promises had reached a point of disappointment and considerable disillusion. The truth is that the very opposite has happened. In all of those fields that I have previously mentioned where the church was expected to exercise such a powerful influence, the decline of decades has not even been arrested; moral deterioration continues and the church which was to have been such a strong influence for good frequently finds itself an object of scorn and ridicule. It has become more than ever marginalised and tends to be thoroughly ignored by government, industry and society in general. I suspect that Restorationism does not have the same dominant place in the churches today as it had then, though it has never been openly repudiated. It has quietly slipped out of prominence. Most of its clearest teachers have either died or have faded from the scene. However, the hunger amongst the people of God for something very spectacular to happen had been born and continues to this day. The great cry was then 'God is doing a new thing' and the momentum has been kept going by new phases with the cry being repeated each time. However, there has still not been any delivery of the expectations.

John Wimber, in 1983, began a process that was to greatly widen this sense of expectation beyond the Restorationist movement. He successfully appealed to the mainline churches, even though he himself is not a 'mainline' man. He taught that signs and wonders allied to evangelism (power evangelism) would lead to great progress in the conversion of the United Kingdom. It did not happen. Strange things undoubtedly did happen in Wimber meetings and particularly during the ministry times as people screamed, fell about and trembled. The momentum was thus maintained. It was felt that something was happening and that it was all going to lead to a great breakthrough for the cause of God.

When in 1990 the Kansas prophets were introduced into the United Kingdom the whole matter of expectations stepped up a gear. It was prophesied that there was going to be a revival later that year which would surpass the revival which had taken place in this nation in the eighteenth century under the Wesleys. Yet again nothing happened, the expectations were not fulfilled and the question undoubtedly arises, how much more can even the most gullible people take of this sort of thing? By this time, undoubtedly, anxiety was at large in charismatic circles. Thus when the Toronto Blessing appeared, the need for something remarkable was so great that the questioning and testing procedures that should always be applied to such things were frankly superficial and sporadic at best. Even though the Toronto Blessing was accompanied by manifestations never before seen in the whole history of the church, including the New Testament record, because something remarkable undoubtedly was happening it has been taken on board in a most indiscriminate manner.

Decline in Bible knowledge

Let me now turn to the second factor which made the charismatic church vulnerable to departure from biblical truth and practice. When the house churches first emerged there was a lot of healthy radical thinking about Christian life and practice. The object of all of this was to endeavour to re-establish something which was perceived to have been lost, namely the simplicity and purity of the life of the early church as depicted in the New Testament. Therefore all church practices were subjected afresh to the scrutiny of God's Word, and I believe that most objective critics would judge that a very great deal of good emerged from that. Even though leaders in the older denominations often saw house churches as a threat, some of them recognised how their own churches might benefit from the discoveries of these new churches.

The search was on for absolute honesty in all aspects of church life and for genuineness in the exercise of charismatic gifts. Anything that was even slightly false was questioned and as an example, house churches were dangerous places to be for anyone wishing to indulge in super-spirituality. Unnecessary meetings were scrapped, along with cumbersome committees, silliness in charismatic things was given short shrift, and ridiculous prophecies were given no houseroom at all. There was the development of genuine fellowship and great generosity, and in the realm of demonology there was no dualism whatsoever; Christ was King over all.

However, in a concerted attack on legalism, diligent application to the Bible itself came under attack, and whether the message was intended or not, large numbers of Christians began a process of taking personal Bible study less and less seriously. At the same time, expository and doctrinal preaching came to be regarded as old hat, intellectualism, heavy and wearisome. As a result there has emerged a famine of the Word of God, and whilst I do not believe that this is confined to the charismatic churches it has nevertheless left large numbers of Christians without the capacity to judge for themselves from Scripture whether a thing is of God or not. They are defenceless against error, both in the form of doctrine and practice, taking hold of the church of God. It even becomes possible for leaders to seriously misquote the Scriptures and the people believe that God is speaking. One video shows Rodney Howard-Browne addressing an audience of thousands who cheer as he declares, 'Don't try to understand this. Don't you know the natural mind cannot receive the things of the Spirit of God.' This is taken from 1 Corinthians 2:14 and is almost a correct quotation. Paul actually says 'the natural *man*' not '*mind*' and he is clearly referring to unregenerate man, non-Christian man. Paul goes on to talk about the Christian man, and asserts that this man has the mind of Christ (v 16 of the same chapter). Such a man is, 'a spiritual man' and is required to judge all things (v 15). What the apostle Paul teaches is the complete opposite of what Browne is saying, and yet Christian people sit there cheering this appalling manipulation of the Word of God.

I am well aware that many people in the Toronto movement are taking steps to put some distance between themselves and Rodney Howard-Browne. Concerning a matter like this, that just will not do. This dictum of Browne's, that is, the by-passing of your mind and your critical faculties, has been carried far and wide into the Toronto Blessing churches and has become a fundamental factor in the whole 'receiving process' of this phenomenon. I quote examples of what has been said in English churches.

> 'Don't let the Bible get in the way of the blessing.'
>
> 'Some of you Bible-lovers need to put it down and let God work on you.'
>
> 'The Bible has let us down. It has not delivered the numbers we need.'
>
> 'You must not let your mind hinder the receiving of the blessing.'

The result of all this is that when a new teaching or a new experience comes along, many Christians have no way of assessing whether or not it is of God. Even when their instincts are telling them 'This is very queer', they jump in just in case it is God at work – they do not want to miss him. If people act in this way, it is inevitable that they will end up in trouble sooner or later, and many well-meaning charismatics have been up one blind alley after another. The dangers are compounded by the fact that too many preacher/leaders have few skills in expounding the Scriptures and laying out the truth before the people. Some hardly speak from the Scriptures at all, and of those who do too many spend their time spiritualising and allegorising them.

The burden of what I am saying is this. Within charismatic churches great expectations have been built up among the people of God; expectations that something spectacular, something extraordinary, something perhaps even sensational is going to happen. Disappointment has followed disappointment, but no one can possibly be satisfied with the simple life of patiently enduring hardship as good soldiers of Jesus Christ, nor faithfully persevering in the face of setbacks, disappointments and defections as the apostles evidently had to; no, there must be something very big round the next corner. But because we live in a day when personal knowledge of the Bible is at its lowest ebb for years, and the capacities for discernment and discrimination have been discarded, the people of God are left wide open to almost anything.

Am I asserting that absolutely nobody in any pro-Toronto church has received any blessing at all from God? No, because God is always eager to bless hungry children who are truly seeking his face and I am therefore in no doubt that there will be individuals who have been truly blessed of God. However, from my own experience, I have to add that it is on nothing like the scale that people would have us believe. There have not been huge numbers of lives remarkably changed, nor have there been large numbers of conversions and nor have there been significant numbers of healings. I shall have more to say about this in the final section.

IS THE TORONTO BLESSING BIBLICAL AND DOES THAT MATTER?

The Toronto Blessing consists of three distinctive parts: the manifestations, the receiving methodology and the claimed testimonies.

The manifestations

I do not propose to spend a great deal of time on this. In Toronto receiving meetings strange things happen; people who are prayed for display unusual behaviour. Falling to the floor and lying supine is almost universal, and laughing uncontrollably almost as widespread. There is a good deal of trembling and jerking, often known as the 'Toronto twitch', weeping and staggering in a seemingly-drunken fashion. Less common, but nonetheless widespread, are many other different physical movements, including certain sorts of dancing and animal movements, and, of course, the notorious animal noises. For the most part all of these things have been declared to be the result of the Holy Spirit being upon people in order to bless them.

When engaged in dialogue about the issue of the Toronto Blessing I have found that all who are supporters of it nevertheless seek to play down the matter of the manifestations. It has been said to me by people that they do not like them but it is necessary to put up with them in order to lay hold of God's best. Even though the whole of the Toronto Blessing is claimed to be a sovereign move of God, the mood amongst the practitioners generally now seems to be to get these particular things under control, which is a strange way to respond to an alleged sovereign act of God. Generally speaking, people who go forward more than once at successive meetings will tend to repeat whatever was the manifestation which they first received. If they became pogo jumpers, for instance, that is probably what they will repeat at future meetings. It is also common for people who are prayed with to receive the specific manifestation which is the characteristic of the person praying for them.

During most of 1994, claims were made that all of

these manifestations could be successfully held up to biblical examination, though I have to say, I have only ever seen attempts to give biblical authentication to the following seven, viz. drunken staggering, losing bodily strength and thus, falling down, laughing uncontrollably, weeping, trembling, lion roaring and convulsions. This last one, convulsions, is a strange odd one out. Gerald Coates wrote in 'Toronto and Scripture' (*Renewal* magazine November 1994), concerning 'manifestations of the Holy Spirit's presence' that 'Scripture gives more than sufficient evidence and endorsement for the following responses'. It becomes the strange odd one out because when he talks about convulsions he says 'most if not all references to do with convulsions have a demonic source'. He proceeds to quote only Mark 1:25–26 and Mark 9:18, both of which are examples of the demonic at work. This matter is in fact doubly strange as Gerald began by declaring he would give 'Scripture . . . endorsement for . . . responses'. Also convulsions, either in the form of strange uncontrollable jerks, or on the floor contraction-like writhings, are very common features of Toronto meetings, and I have never seen or heard of any being declared demonic. Around the world at conferences and in papers, the claims that these things were biblical were strongly challenged. I do not propose here to repeat the basis of that challenge because the attempt to biblically vindicate, such as it was, has now been largely withdrawn. Late in 1994, the Vineyard International Council, a body which has some oversight of the churches which relate to John Wimber, made the following statement which was reported in *Alpha* magazine:

> We are willing to allow experiences to happen without endorsing, encouraging or stimulating them; nor should we seek to explain them by

> inappropriate proof-texting. Biblical metaphors (similar to those concerning a lion or dove, etc.) do not justify or provide a proof text for animal behaviour . . . The point is, don't try to defend unusual manifestations from biblical texts that *obviously lack a one to one correspondence with a current experience*. (Emphasis mine.)

I can only presume that this is a complete retraction of what was said in the earlier days. For example, in May 1994, Bill Jackson of the Vineyard Champagne Church, Illinois, produced a paper which was subsequently widely circulated and entitled, 'What in the world is happening to us?'. In his introduction he says, 'Our purpose in putting this paper together is to develop *a biblical apologetic* for what we see happening among us. Much of what we are seeing is strange to the natural mind.' That paper was issued to leaders who went to the Airport Vineyard Church, Toronto, and was then well used by them in their own churches in this country. The proponents have now clearly conceded that there is no biblical foundation for these manifestations. I am in little doubt that no concession would have been made were it not for the fact that lots of us who are profoundly troubled by these things had made a very strong challenge about the feeble biblical ground the claims stood on. Without that challenge, for the reasons that I have already given, thousands of ordinary Christians would have continued in the delusion that it was all thoroughly biblical.

However, that is not the end of the debate, because that same Vineyard International Council effectively now asserts that a biblical basis is not needed for such things. And I quote again:

> The absence of proof texts does not disallow an experience. If so none of us would, a) go to Dis-

neyland, b) use computers, c) have worship bands.

All Christians ought to find a statement like this at very least surprising if not outrageous. How anyone can dare to say that we need no more biblical justification for something that is supposed to be a great move of God than we need for going to Disneyland, is completely outside the range of my whole Christian experience. As this issue of what needs biblical justification and what does not is dealt with elsewhere in this book, I will take this matter no further. Sufficient for me to say that it is now acknowledged there is no biblical basis for these strange things, even though they have been a fundamental part of the whole Toronto experience.

We are not at the end of our problems with these manifestations. Many of its advocates now acknowledge that there is, 'a lot of flesh' and some demonic activity. In other words they are saying 'there is something wrong'. But I have to draw attention to a number of things concerning these new statements.

They do not go on to eradicate that which is of the flesh, or the demonic.

They do not even go on to identify it.

For most of 1994 it was emphatically declared to be the Holy Spirit at work, all of it.

Manifestations accelerate and get stronger when the one ministering cries such things as, 'More Lord', or wafts his hand towards the receiver. I ask myself what kind of Lord do they suppose they are appealing to, who will give them control of that sort over another believer? I further ask, what kind of Christian would want to have that kind of control? Instead of being disturbed by this, many in this movement rejoice that, as they suppose, God is using them.

If they do find manifestations which are wrong after all, what are they going to do with the 'prophetic' interpretations which accompanied them. When someone roared like a lion, it was said that manhood was being restored to the church; a man, cock-a-doodle-dooing was God saying 'Church wake up!'; when young girls danced as round a totem pole, God was giving them a warrior spirit, and if your feet became hot there was God giving you the gift of evangelism. There have been many other such prophetic interpretations.

The receiving methodology

The claim is widely made that via Toronto receiving meetings people go on to experience great advance in the realm of sanctification. It is claimed that people are moving into areas of very significant holiness where besetting sins previously dominated.

As has been shown earlier in this chapter, the style of receiving methodology is not new in the charismatic movement. It has prevailed for years and therefore will come as no surprise to thousands of Christians. What I am going on to say may well produce a reaction of 'So what? Who cares? The whole thing works so does anything else matter?'

First of all, yet again, the New Testament, indeed the whole Bible, never gives an example of meetings being convened for the laying on of hands, resulting in Christian people being significantly more sanctified. None of the Bible's teaching on sanctification so much as hints that procedures like this could help. Yet here we are being presented with this method as the great thing that God is doing today.

The second point at issue is that the New Testament does most clearly tell us how sanctification will come about. In John 17:17–20 Jesus is praying to his Father for his people and he says '[Father] sanctify them by the truth; your word is truth'. He had previously taught in John 15:3, 'Now you are clean through the word which I have spoken to you'. Paul taught in 2 Timothy 3:16–17, 'All Scripture is . . . useful for teaching, rebuking, correcting and training in righteousness, so that the man of God may be thoroughly equipped for every good work'. When Paul addresses his farewells to the Ephesian elders in Acts 20, he says in verse 32, 'Now I commit you to God and to the word of his grace, which can build you up and give you an inheritance among all those who are sanctified'. We have very similar teaching in the Old Testament, for example, Psalm 119:11, 'I have hidden your word in my heart that I might not sin against you'.

What are all these scriptures saying? They are telling us very plainly that sanctification, cleansing and living in righteousness come to the people of God through the Word of God, that is, through the Scriptures. It is necessary to feed on the Scriptures, to meditate upon them, to digest them, to absorb them and hide them away in our hearts. Through them we learn to respond to God's disciplines and to benefit from them; we learn to trust in God working out his purposes in times of turmoil and trial and tribulation. Supremely we discover who God is, that is, his nature and his character and we will read over and over again how much he supports us and how much he has done for us, and indeed, is doing for us. We shall become familiar with the full revelation of God in the Lord Jesus Christ, whom we look to in order to lay aside every weight, and the sin which so easily besets us. This is the pattern set for us in the New Testament. It is the Lord Jesus himself and the apostles who have taught all of this and we surely finish up at odds with them if in these last years of the twentieth century we go down a different route altogether.

The Bible is clear that we can be converted in a moment following repentance from sin and faith in the Lord Jesus; it is equally clear that the work of sanctification takes a lifetime. It is a consequence of the Holy Spirit working in the life of the believer, through the ministry of the Word of God, as shown above. In Ephesians 5:26 Paul teaches that Christ will sanctify and cleanse the church which he loves with 'the washing with water *through the word*' in order to ultimately present to himself a glorious church, not having spot or wrinkle or any such thing. We will take this matter a little further in the next section.

The claimed testimonies

There are those who claim that, as a result of the type of ministry I have described, they have had an experience of God resulting in a new love for the Lord Jesus Christ, a new love for the Scriptures, increased zeal in witnessing and freedom from besetting sins. These are very significant claims.

However, these claims are made – and accepted – very soon after the ministry experience from which they are said to result. No experienced and responsible pastor would allow such a situation to arise. Proper pastoral responsibility to those who believe they have had an experience of God does not involve only the offering of encouragement and support; it also involves ensuring that spiritual progress is maintained and also determining whether the experience stands the test of time.

It is irresponsible to give instant public prominence to someone who believes he has had such an experience, and this for two reasons. Firstly, it does not allow the experience to be tested. Secondly, public applause is the worst possible environment for spiritual growth. Many Toronto leaders are not without pastoral experience. Why then are they allowing this?

I believe the reason is that sanctification – love of God, love of Scripture etc. – is demonstrably biblical, whilst all other features of the Toronto Blessing are not. These testimonies are, in fact, being used to authenticate the Toronto Blessing as a whole, the argument being that if the Toronto Blessing results in sanctification, it must be of God and so therefore must its manifestations and methodology.

But does it result in sanctification? As I have said, no time is being allowed for testing the claims; testimonies are accepted long before anyone can be sure that there will be permanent fruit. We are being asked to accept these testimonies as genuine in order that we might also accept the Toronto Blessing as genuine, with all that this implies. This is no light matter. We are surely entitled to ask that the testimonies be proved over time before being presented as evidence. I have heard of many claims of changed lives, but my own knowledge of the people concerned does not support these claims.

I know many people who have accepted the Toronto Blessing; most of them I have known for many years. Before they became involved in the Toronto Blessing the majority were agreeable and amiable Christians, and they remain so; but I do not note startling changes in them. Others were less agreeable before their Toronto experience and unfortunately they also have not changed. Many of both groups report pleasant experiences of 'carpet time', but I detect no fundamental changes of the sort that are being claimed. To me, of course, this comes as no surprise, in view of the general absence of the Word of God within the Toronto Blessing.

We may hope that there are some who, because of their genuine and earnest seeking of God, have truly met with him and received blessing at his hand. But before we can accept the huge claims of widespread personal renewal, we must have solid evidence which meets the standards of Scripture and stands the test of time.

CONCLUSION

I feel strongly that the reservations I have set out in this chapter need to be heeded. The Bible must be restored to the position of honour which it formerly had within the evangelical tradition. Unless this happens there is no knowing where Christianity will end up.

Some supporters of the Toronto Blessing object to this emphasis on Scripture on the grounds that it circumscribes God's actions. God, they argue, must be allowed to work in any way he chooses. I fully endorse this latter point, but we must recognise that one of the things God has chosen to do is to give us responsibility for testing things. He has also chosen to give us in the Scriptures an account of his character and his ways, thereby equipping us with the means of testing whether or not something is of him.

Scripture contains many warnings, both from the apostles and from the Lord Jesus Christ himself, concerning the danger of deception and counterfeit works. Some of these will be so subtly disguised as to deceive the very elect. We are exhorted to watch, to test, to be on our guard, and to examine all things; and to be ready to reject those things which fail the test.

The church must return to the Bible as the supreme authority in faith and practice. As I said at the beginning of this chapter we are in a battle for the Bible. We must reassert its sufficiency as a criterion for judging all things. What possible grounds can there be for thinking that now, at the end of the twentieth century, God is introducing any other?

CHAPTER FOUR

'FROM NORTH BATTLEFORD TO TORONTO'

An Examination of the influence of the 1948 North American 'Latter Rain Revival' Movement

Due to unusual events and a new teaching propounded in the preceding eighteen months, in the autumn of 1949, at the 23rd General Council meeting of the Assemblies of God in the USA, held in Seattle, Washington, the following resolution was passed by an overwhelming majority:

> OFFICIAL DISAPPROVAL OF THE 'NEW ORDER OF THE LATTER RAIN'
> WHEREAS, We are grateful for the visitation of God in the past and the evidences of His blessings upon us today, and
> WHEREAS, We recognise a hunger on the part of God's people for a spiritual refreshing and manifestation of His Holy Spirit, be it therefore
> RESOLVED, That we disapprove of these extreme teachings and practices, which, being unfounded Scripturally, serve only to break fel-

lowship of like precious faith and tend to confusion and division among the members of the Body of Christ, and be it hereby known that this 23rd General Council disapproves of the so-called 'New Order of the Latter Rain' to wit:

1. The overemphasis relative to imparting, identifying, bestowing or confirming of gifts by the laying on of hands and prophecy.
2. The erroneous teaching that the Church is built on the foundation of present-day apostles and prophets.
3. The extreme teaching as advocated by the 'New Order' regarding the confession of sin to man and deliverance as practiced, which claims prerogatives to human agency which belong only to Christ.
4. The erroneous teaching concerning the impartation of the gifts of languages as special equipment for missionary service.
5. The extreme and unscriptural practice of imparting or imposing personal leadings by the means of gifts of utterance.
6. Such other wrestings and distortions of Scripture interpretations which are in opposition to teachings and practices generally accepted among us.

BE IT FURTHER RESOLVED, That we recommend following those things which make for peace among us, and those doctrines and practices whereby we may edify one another, endeavouring to keep the unity of the Spirit until we all come into the unity of faith.

This resolution of the Pentecostal Assemblies was occasioned by the fact that some eighteen months earlier, on 12 February 1948, the so-called 'Latter Rain Revival' had begun at the Sharon Bible School in

North Battleford, Saskatchewan, Canada. This 'revival' began among about seventy students who, when their names had been prophetically revealed as being 'ready to receive', manifested 'gifts' after being 'prayed over' and having hands laid upon them by the school leadership.

George Hawtin and his brother Ern, together with P.G. Hunt (who along with George had recently resigned as a pastor in the Pentecostal Assemblies of Canada) and the Hawtin's brother-in-law, Milford Kirkpatrick, had some six months earlier joined the Rev Herrick Holt of the Saskatchewan Church of the Foursquare Gospel in an independent work called 'Sharon Orphanage and Schools'.[1] Together they opened Sharon Bible School on 21 October 1947.

The Pentecostal movement, which had began with the Azusa Street revival in San Francisco in 1906, had by this time been going for over forty years and much of its denominational life had become quite ritualised. It had lost its spontaneity and much of the use of the gifts or manifestations of the Holy Spirit in regular church life had become merely theoretical. Since the mid-1930s there had existed a deep spiritual hunger in many Pentecostals for some kind of revival of the spiritual energy and enthusiasm, accompanied by the manifestations of the Holy Spirit's presence, that had characterised their beginnings.

EARLY PRECURSORS TO THE 'LATTER RAIN'

There were two men in particular whose teaching and ministry greatly influenced those through whom the Latter Rain movement started.

Franklin Hall

The men who started the Sharon Bible School were all looking for some kind of revival. Herrick Holt had been preaching for some time that God was going to do a 'new thing' in accordance with Isaiah 43:18–19, although he was still awaiting revelation from the Holy Spirit as to what the 'new thing' would be.[2] Their expectations of revival were heightened and much influenced by a book entitled *Atomic Power with God through Fasting and Prayer*, written by one Franklin Hall in 1946. Hall was an ex-Methodist who had begun an independent travelling evangelistic and healing ministry. In the autumn of 1946 he had set up in San Diego, California what he called 'a major fasting and prayer daily revival center'.[3] However, Hall was very much into his own brand of theology. He was convinced that the church was on the brink of a great worldwide revival, and that from this revival would emerge a victorious, perfected church which would include the 'overcomers' who would attain immortality. One of his particular teachings was that fasting was the primary means by which revival would come and bring in the restoration of the church. He maintained that God always responded to fasting and that without fasting, prayer was ineffectual. However, he also maintained that all prayer, if accompanied by fasting, was effective irrespective of to whom it was made. By way of proof of this assertion, Hall would quote that the American Indian tribes had their prayers to the Great Spirit answered because they fasted.[4] According to Hall, during the first year of ministry in the revival centre, there were over one thousand people who claimed to have been converted, with many testifying to having been healed of various sicknesses and diseases through fasting and prayer. He also claimed actual appearances of the Holy Spirit in fire and smoke.[5]

Hall also taught that the restoration of the church would involve the immortality of believers in the Lord Jesus by means of stages of spiritual growth. This would be achieved through a life of holiness plus various psycho-spiritual encounters (i.e. experiences with UFOs, UHOs – unidentified heavenly objects – and IHOs – immortal heavenly objects).[6] He called this 'overcoming' which would bring a 'rain of righteousness' or 'a rain of immortality' upon the earth and revitalise the sleeping church.[7] Hall also taught a number of other strange and non-biblical doctrines including assigning spiritual significance to the signs of the zodiac. He believed that what he was encouraging was all part of the fulfilment of the Joel's Army prophecy of Joel 2:3–11 when 'gravity freed, great people will run up walls' and 'permanent, lasting Freedoms from all sickness, harmful, accident things and defeat will come about' in this present life. He even went as far as to teach that 'Freedom from the imprisonment of all gravitational forces will also be brought upon the whole man. This study teaches one the power and secrets of space flight . . . It gives the Bible formula for weightlessness, the "raising up" power of those who come to immortality (Jn 6 and Rom 2:7)'.[8]

Despite his obviously aberrant beliefs and his works-orientated methodology with its possibly occult overtones, Franklin Hall's book was a great success and brought him some fame. Not only was it a great influence upon the Sharon Bible School brothers but others in the 'healing evangelism' stream such as Gordon Lindsay, Oral Roberts and William Branham claimed to be much influenced by its teaching. No one seems to have been in the least concerned about Hall's non-biblical beliefs and practices and simply accepted his fasting methods, presumably on some kind of pragmatic basis.

William Branham

The Sharon brothers were also considerably impressed with the ministry of William Branham and they attended a 'healing campaign' meeting that Branham was holding in Vancouver only three months before the Sharon 'revival' began.[9] It is said that some of them had Branham lay hands on them for the impartation of spiritual power.

William Branham was born near Burkesville, Kentucky on 6 April 1909 and his various biographers say that miraculous visitations and supernatural events followed him from birth. For example, one of his biographers, Pearry Green, relates that a visible light hovered over his crib the day he was born, accompanied by what he calls 'a strange aura, a Presence'.[10] It is also claimed that he received his first vision at the age of three and that at the age of seven had his first experience of what he called 'the voice' which told him, 'Never smoke, drink nor defile your body, for when you are older there is a work for you to do'.[11] During 1933 Branham had a series of seven visions regarding forthcoming major events that would take place in the world. This led him to predict (he was at pains to stress that it was not a prophecy)[12] that the end of this present age – which he equated with the Laodicean Church – would occur around 1977 and the millennium would then begin. Although it could be said that there has been quite substantial fulfilment of Branham's first six visions, the last and final vision, which he saw as occurring in 1977, and involved the physical destruction of America, has not yet come to pass.[13]

His national healing ministry began in the spring of 1946. According to his own testimony God led him to a secret cave (some versions of his biography say a cabin) in Indiana on 7 May of that year where he met an 'angel' who told him 'Fear not! I am a messenger, sent unto you from the presence of Almighty God. I want you to know that your strange life has been for a purpose in preparing you to do a job that God has ordained for you to do from your birth. If you will be sincere, and you can get the people to believe you, nothing will stand before your prayer, not even cancer'.[14] The angel then went on to tell him that it would be necessary for people to confess their sins before they appeared before him for ministry and that he would be used to preach to multitudes all over the world in packed auditoriums. According to Pearry Green the angel told Branham of 'a fabulous ministry to take place'.[15] Branham also alleges that the 'angel' (whom he appears to have identified with 'the voice') told him that he would be able to detect diseases by vibrations in his left hand and have the ability to tell people's secret thoughts. Branham said that the 'angel' always accompanied him on stage at his healing sessions and stood at his side, and he is also on record as saying that the healings were not done by him but by his 'angel'.[16] Branham put great store on the direction given to him by this 'angel', even cancelling meetings because of what the 'angel' told him.

Branham held his first 'healing revival' meeting in St Louis in June 1946 and his reputation soon spread. According to David Harrell Jr, who wrote a history of the healing and charismatic revivals in America entitled *All Things Are Possible*, 'Branham's healing power became a worldwide legend: there were continued reports that he raised the dead'.[17] It was said that Branham's ability to discern people's illnesses, and sometimes their sins, although he had never seen them before, was amazing. Ern Baxter, who was a member of Branham's team and worked with him for between four and eight months every year for six years, said that he never once saw Branham's discernment miss, and the Pentecostal historian Walter J. Hollenweger, who knew Branham personally and interpreted for him on his visits to Switzerland, wrote of 'Branham's ability to name with astonishing accuracy the sickness, and often also the hidden sins, of people whom he had never seen'. Hollenweger also said that he was 'not aware of any case in which he was mistaken in the often detailed statements he made'. Significantly, however, he also says, 'By contrast to what he claimed, only a small percentage of those who sought healing were in fact healed.'[18]

Branham was convinced that the church was on the edge of restoration and the manifestation of God's kingdom on earth, basing much of his teaching on the scriptures of Joel 2:23 and Revelation 1:20–3:22. He interpreted the 'latter rain' of Joel 2 as the new Pentecostalism of his day and taught that God was restoring his church from what he called 'the locusts of denominationalism' or 'the mark of the beast'. From the passage in Revelation he taught that 'God's Seventh Church Age' (i.e. the Laodicean age) had come and identified it as God's final move. He claimed that the angels (or messengers) to the seven churches were simply men who appeared at particular times in church history to bring new revelation to lead the church progressively to sanctification. Many saw Branham as the messenger to the end-time Laodicean church and hailed him as the greatest apostle and prophet for the final age of the church. For example, Paul Cain, who at that time exercised a 'healing evangelism' ministry and had considerable association with Branham, described him as 'the greatest prophet of the twentieth century'.[19] *Voice*, the magazine of the FGBMI, went further and said 'In Bible Days, there were men of God who were Prophets and Seers. But in all the Sacred records, none of these had a greater ministry than that of William Branham.'[20]

However, like Franklin Hall, Branham had some decidedly non-orthodox theological views, especially about the doctrine of the Trinity. He did not accept the orthodox teaching of a Godhead comprising of the Three Persons of Father, Son and Holy Spirit which he said was the 'Babylonian Foundation' of denominationalism. Rather, like the heresy of Arianism, he believed in one Godhead which showed itself in the three 'attributes' of Father, Son and Holy Spirit. He also espoused the view that God had given his word not only in the Bible but also in the Zodiac and the pyramids of Egypt. These aberrant beliefs, together with his unorthodox ministry methods, eventually brought Branham into conflict, first with the Pentecostal Assemblies of Canada, and eventually with other main-line denominations. However, as in the case of Franklin Hall, there were those who were prepared to totally overlook Branham's aberrant theology for the sake of the signs and wonders of his ministry. For example, many in the 'healing evangelism' stream did so on the basis of 'unity' which was for them an important issue. Gordon Lindsay, who was seen as the co-ordinator of the healing movement, is said to have 'repeatedly stressed' the need for a 'vision of the unity of God's people'. He is reported also to have said of Branham that 'the uniting of believers had been the burden of his heart from the time that the angel had visited him'.

The brothers from Sharon were very affected by what they experienced at the Branham meeting in Vancouver. This is clear from a glowing article which appeared in the January 1948 issue of their periodical *The Sharon Star*:

The Branham Campaign in Vancouver B.C. was a

> great success.... Never in my life have I seen anything to equal what I saw in Vancouver... His [Branham's] sermons have the effect of inspiring faith in his hearers.... To my best knowledge I did not see one person who was not healed when brother Branham took time to pray specially for him.... I came home from those meetings realising as never before that the real gifts of the Holy Spirit are far mightier than we have imagined in our wildest dreams.... All great outpourings of the past have had their outstanding truths. Luther's truth was Justification by Faith. Wesley's was Sanctification. The Baptists taught the premillenial coming of Christ. The Missionary Alliance taught Divine Healing. The Pentecostal outpouring has restored the Baptism of the Holy Ghost to its rightful place. But the next great outpouring is going to be marked by all these other truths plus a demonstration of the nine gifts of the Spirit as the world, not even the Apostolic world, has ever witnessed before. This revival will be short and will be the last before the Rapture of the Church.[21]

Branham differed from the other healing evangelists of his day in that he linked healing with the casting out of demons and one of his ministry methods was to cast out a demon by the laying on of hands, so that a miraculous healing might follow. In his MA thesis to the University of Manitoba, 'The Pentecostal Movement', C. J. Jaenen suggests that Branham's use of the laying on of hands in his healing campaigns influenced the Sharon brothers to do the same in their subsequent ministry.[22] This question of the use of the laying on of hands was the first issue to bring the emerging Latter Rain movement into conflict with the Pentecostal Assemblies.

THE RAIN DESCENDS

As already stated, the Sharon group were much affected by the teaching of Franklin Hall on fasting. Ern Hawtin wrote in his account of the beginnings of the 'Latter Rain Revival':

> The truth of fasting was one great contributing factor to the revival. One year before this we had read Franklin Hall's book, entitled 'Atomic Power with God Through Fasting and Prayer'. We immediately began to practise fasting. Previously we had not understood the possibility of long fasts. The revival would never have been possible without the restoration of this great truth through our good brother Hall.[23]

However he fails to give any biblical reasoning or explanation of 'this great truth' and how it brought revival.

So having returned from the Branham meeting they decided to put Franklin Hall's teaching into practice and according to George Hawtin, 'Some fasted for 3 days; some for 7 days; some fasted for 10 days; some 2 weeks; some for 3 weeks; some fasted for 30 days; and one man fasted for 40 days'.

It was not however until February that the long-awaited revival arrived. On 11 February, one of the Bible School young ladies prophesied 'saying that we were on the very verge of a great revival, and that all we had to do was open the door, and we could enter in'. When she had finished prophesying, George Hawtin rose and prayed 'beseeching God and telling him that he had informed us that we were on the very verge of a great revival, and all we had to do was enter the door – but George Hawtin said, "Father, we do not know where the door is, neither do we know how to enter it" '.

The following day, 12 February, was described by Ern Hawtin as follows in his report *How this Revival Began*:

> . . . I shall never forget the morning that God moved into our midst in this strange new manner. Some students were under the power of God on the floor, others were kneeling in adoration and worship before the Lord. The anointing deepened until the awe of God was upon everyone. The Lord spoke to one of the brethren, 'Go and lay hands upon a certain student and pray for him'. While he was in doubt and contemplation one of the sisters who had been under the power of God went to the brother saying the same words, and naming the identical student he was to pray for. He went in obedience and the revelation was given concerning the student's life and future ministry. After this a long prophecy was given [by Ern Hawtin] with minute details concerning the great thing God was about to do. The pattern for the revival and many details concerning it were given. To this day [his report was written 1 August 1949] I can remember the gist of the prophecy, 'These are the last days, my people. The coming of the Lord draweth nigh, and I shall move in the midst of mine own. The gifts of the Spirit will be restored to my church. If thou shalt obey me I shall immediately restore them. But Oh my people I would have you to be reverent before me as never before. Take the shoes off thy feet for the ground on which thou standest is holy. If thou dost not reverence the Lord and his House, the Lord shall require it at thy hands. Do not speak lightly of the things I am about to do for the Lord shall not hold thee guiltless. Do not gossip about these things. Do not write letters to

> thy nearest friends, of the new way in which the Lord moveth, for they will not understand. If thou dost disobey the Lord in these things take heed lest thy days be numbered in sorrow and thou goest early to the grave. Thou hast obeyed me and I shall restore my gifts to you. I shall indicate from time to time those who are to receive the gifts of my Spirit. They shall be received by prophecy and the laying on of hands of the presbytery.'
>
> Immediately following this prophecy a sister who was under the power of God gave by revelation the names of five students who were ready to receive. Hands were laid upon them by the presbytery. This procedure was very faltering and imperfect that morning but after two days searching the word of God to see if we were on scriptural grounds, great unity prevailed and the Lord came forth in greater power and glory day by day. Soon a visible manifestation of gifts was received when candidates were prayed over, and many as a result began to be healed as gifts of healing were received. Day after day the glory and power of God came amongst us. Great repentance, humbling, fasting and prayer prevailed in everyone.[24]

Ern Hawtin's prophecy stated that 'the gifts of the Spirit will be restored to my church'. Although one of the main marks of the advent of Pentecostalism at the turn of the century was the manifestation and operation of the gifts of the Spirit, there had been a general falling away of the use of these gifts amongst the Pentecostal churches, and this lack had been recognised. It was this lack that brought the events at North Battleford into the limelight. Because the North Battleford brothers were successful in imparting spiritual gifts by the laying on of their hands, people came from all across Canada and the United States to their meetings so that they, too, might partake of these spiritual gifts for which many of them had long been praying.

As mentioned at the start of this chapter, the leadership of the Pentecostal denominations were not prepared to accept that the baptism and gifts of the Holy Spirit could be imparted by the laying on of hands. For nearly fifty years they had clung to the methodology of the Azusa Street revival in which 'tarrying' or waiting for the coming of the Holy Spirit on one's life was practised (Acts 1:4). Ernest S. Williams, who was General Superintendent of the Assemblies of God at that time, said, 'Concerning the nine gifts spoken of in 1 Corinthians 12, if you will carefully read the account I think you will discern that they each come directly from God's sovereign bestowment; I do not find any record where they are to be bestowed by means of an intermediate channel'. Of course if one reads the record of the Acts of the Apostles we find that no one methodology was used as far as receiving the baptism in the Holy Spirit is concerned (Acts 2:4; 8:17; 10:44). However we need to remember that the question of formulae and methods in ministry, including the use of the laying on of hands, has never been adequately resolved in the charismatic movement.

THE MOVEMENT SPREADS

In keeping with the injunction in the prophecy over publishing news of the 'revival', the March issue of *The Sharon Star* contained no news of what had happened, but an editorial on the subject appeared in the April issue. This published report undoubtedly played a large part in attracting a larger than usual number to the 1948 Annual Feast of Pentecost camp meeting. Its front page had also carried headlines reporting 'Two Modern Miracles' involving healing at Sharon Bible College.

There were many testimonies from pastors across the country as to how God had empowered them during their time at the camp meetings so that it had revolutionised their home churches and by May, 1948, parallels were already being drawn with the earlier Pentecostal revival of 1906. George Hawtin suspected that 'revival is breaking out among small groups all over America and no doubt in other countries as well'. There were certainly reports from Norway that some kind of revival was taking place among Pentecostals at that time.

Hawtin also noted that the restoration of the gifts of the Spirit was the result of God giving 'new revelation' of truth from the Scriptures. He wrote that 'great revivals always are accompanied by some present truth when old light is rediscovered . . .'.[25] It soon became a prominent idea in the movement and created an expectation that the Lord would continue to reveal new truth from the Scriptures. This belief in a new wave of the progressive revelation of scriptural truth through prophecy became widespread and has continued to be a pervasive influence in charismatic churches, thousands of which have adopted various ideas that became prominent in the ministry of the North Battleford brethren.

As in the case of Branham and the healing evangelists, the Sharon group were keen to stress their concerns for unity. Reg Layzell, who was one of seven men 'ordained' by the Sharon leadership to exercise an 'apostolic ministry' on behalf of the 'Presbytery' but who subsequently became disillusioned to the extent that he disassociated himself from them said, following the camp meeting of July 1948, 'The great message that stirred all souls was first the message of the Body of Christ coming together',[26] and George Warnock noted in the preface to the first edition of *The Feast of Tabernacles*, that 'God came forth in answer to the prayer and fasting of his children, poured out the gifts of the Holy Spirit, and revealed the fact that now at this time He would bring His body together, and make His Church one glorious Church without spot or wrinkle'.[27]

However, the problem was that 'unity' always appeared to depend upon an acceptance of the teachings and practices which they as God's specially anointed apostles and prophets were now revealing. This of course was not biblical. The Scriptures plainly teach that the foundation of our unity lies in our relationship by faith with the Lord Jesus. It is maintained by our daily obedience to the precepts and teachings recorded for us in the Scriptures. Paul refers to this in his first letter to the Corinthian believers (1 Cor 11:2) and Jude exhorts us to 'contend for the faith that was once for all entrusted to the saints' (Jude 3).

Another point of controversy that arose at that time between the North Battleford group and the leaders of the Pentecostal denominations was the former's insistence that the church had present-day apostles and prophets. The first indication of this controversy appeared in the 1 June 1948 issue of *The Sharon Star* when George Hawtin wrote: 'When one starts talking about prophets and apostles being in the Church in our day, the poor saints are shocked half to death. They raise their hands in holy terror and cry, "heresy, heresy!" '

However, the point of controversy with the Pentecostal denominations was not simply the question *per se* of 'prophets and apostles being in the church in our day'. There is undoubtedly a vital place in the church for the ministry of apostles and prophets as mentioned in Ephesians 4:11, but the issue was, and remains, whether this or any other scripture allows us to conclude that God has now raised up within the church 'special' apostles and prophets through whom he gives extra-biblical revelation and the power of extraordinary signs and wonders to guide and direct his people in these 'last days'.

Also appearing in the June issue of *The Sharon Star* was the statement that 'no church exercises or has any right to exercise authority or jurisdiction over another, its pastors or members'.

This statement did nothing to help the Sharon group's growing estrangement from the main Pentecostal denominations and would have been more helpful had Hawtin applied it to the excesses of authoritarianism and elitism that later developed in connection with the 'travelling presbytery' from North Battleford, of which he was a part and which was accused of exercising considerable authority over people in other church situations by means of directive prophecy.

During 7–18 July 1948, thousands of people throughout the North American continent, having heard of the North Battleford awakening, flocked to the Sharon Camp Meeting held there at that time. It had been preceded by a week of fasting and prayer from 27 June to 4 July which had also been widely attended. Among those attending was George Warnock, who had earlier, for two or three years, been personal secretary to Ern Baxter. It was at this time that he heard James Watt, one of the teachers at the Camp Meeting, casually mention that the third of Israel's great feasts, the Feast of Tabernacles, had not yet been fulfilled. According to Warnock: 'I somehow never forgot that, and over the period of a year or more following this, the message seemed to grow on me as I read the Scriptures . . . James certainly dropped a seed in my heart when he spoke of the Feast of Tabernacles . . .'.[28]

In July, 1951, Sharon Publishers printed George Warnock's book, *The Feast of Tabernacles* which became a major doctrinal work of the Latter Rain movement.

Warnock's thesis is that the three great annual feasts of the Lord in Israel's worship, which are set out in considerable detail in Leviticus and Deuteronomy, pre-figure and typify the whole church age beginning with the cross and consummating in the manifestation of the sons of God (explained further on p 83) and the glorious display of God's power and glory. There is of course truth in much of Warnock's work, because there is a real sense in which we can see Israel's feasts as a pre-figure of events in the New Testament. For example, Pentecost and the coming of the Holy Spirit and obviously Passover and the death of Jesus. But what about the Feast of Tabernacles? Warnock's proposal is that the Feast of Tabernacles is analogous to what he called 'the manifestation of the sons of God' (Rom 8). He taught that the church needed to be restored. The church was weak, the church was diseased, the church was totally defeated, the church was ineffective and needed restoration. According to Warnock that restoration would be done in one particular way. He states clearly that all the orthodox understanding about restoration should be discarded. Restoration will not come through reading the Bible, will not come from praying, and will not come through fasting. It will only come through the aegis of God's apostles and prophets. This of course was one of the assertions of the Hawtin brothers. God would restore his church through his newly-appointed apostles and prophets, who of course included themselves. In similar vein they were also the presbytery through whose hands God's new blessings of power and gifting were to be received. Warnock therefore taught that God was raising up new apostles and prophets and that they would restore the church; they would bring the church into perfection, and they would bring the church into – he never actually used the word 'immortality' – but said they would bring forth a church which would never know disease, which would never die, and so on. This of course brings us back full circle to Franklin Hall.

These teachings are from the 'new revelation of truth' stream which became so prominent in the Latter Rain movement and which has continued to dog the charismatic movement throughout its history. No honest examination of the biblical text can substantiate these eschatological extravagances. Acts chapter one records that the Lord Jesus will physically return to earth as he physically left it and the Apostle Paul made it quite clear that he would be released from 'this body of death' only at the Lord's return. It would be then that he would change 'our lowly bodies so that they will be like his glorious body' (Phil 3:21). Likewise the Apostle John tells us that 'when he appears, we shall be like him' (1 John 3:2).

THE MOVEMENT IN DECLINE

The influence of the Sharon group soon began to wane, largely because of the increasing criticism of their methods and practices. As early as November 1948, *The Sharon Star* contains an article by Ern Hawtin which appears to be in response to the growing unease and in it he complains that 'whenever God sends a revival, the enemy, who is the author of confusion, will move, either to hinder its progress, or force its followers into some extreme, that its power might become a reproach to the world or the Church'. The main accusations being made against the Sharon group concerned their authoritarianism and their insistence that only they, or those appointed by them, had the right to lay on hands for the reception of spiritual gifts and also their growing tendency to try to influence fellowships and individuals through directive prophecy. They were also accused of allowing novices to prophesy, and general spiritual fanaticism. However, others who had attended the Sharon meetings in North Battleford took the Latter Rain message to many of the North American cities during 1948 and 1949. Many pastors left their denominations as a result and independent churches began to spring up across the continent. It is interesting to note that in 1950 George Hawtin, who by this time was no longer a major figure in the movement, wrote, in the September issue of *The Sharon Star*, 'A few weeks ago I was presented with a list of almost one hundred LATTER RAIN CHURCHES. I do not know where the list came from, though my own name was upon it . . . this is fundamentally and foundationally and scripturally WRONG'.

As the 1950s progressed the Latter Rain movement began to lose its high profile although undoubtedly many continued to follow its various beliefs and practices in independent churches across the North American continent. Its influence did move outside North America, largely perhaps because at a Convention held in October 1950 in Toronto, leaders were encouraged to take the 'Latter Rain' message abroad. As a result various leaders visited India, East Africa, Ethiopia, Japan, New Zealand, and various countries in Europe.

It is difficult to gauge how far the Latter Rain movement impacted the church in England beyond its introduction into the Apostolic Church. Cecil Cousen and George Evans, pastors in the Apostolic Church in the UK had gone to North America in 1949 where they both became involved. However, Cecil Cousen appears to have been wary of the Sharon group since while stating that 'the Latter Rain was a real move of the Spirit' also said that 'the Hawtin brothers very quickly got into very strange doctrines'.[29] Fred Poole, who was an Apostolic Church pastor who had emigrated to North America from South Wales during World War II and had become superintendent of the Apostolic Church in the United States in 1947, also became an active proponent of the Latter Rain movement. Cousen, Evans and Poole all returned to England during the course of 1951 and ministered at a Council Meeting of the Apostolic Church in Bradford. Cecil Cousen's report on that meeting was that 'the people accepted the Latter Rain ministry with open hearts . . . People were baptised in the Spirit, many were healed and filled with the Spirit and demons were cast out, and the blessing of the Lord was there . . .' Fred Poole recorded that

> The brethren had heard many things about this Latter Rain visitation, but as we gave them first-hand news of what God . . . has done in our own hearts, there was a melting, a breaking and a crying, as the Spirit witnessed to our simple word of testimony . . . Latter Rain choruses . . . were quickly learned and sung, both in council and public services, the Spirit bearing testimony to the precious truths of this 'end-time' visitation.

There was much controversy in the Apostolic Church as a whole over the Latter Rain which led eventually to Cecil Cousen being asked to resign as an Apostolic pastor. He went on to become a prominent leader in the charismatic renewal movement in Britain and wielded considerable influence within the Fountain Trust.

THE MANIFEST SONS OF GOD MOVEMENT

Increasingly many Latter Rain followers went underground as some of the leaders began to promote more and more spiritual excesses. Much of the excess had to do with the Manifest Sons of God movement. First set out by George Warnock in his book *The Feast of Tabernacles*, it was obviously being taught much earlier by some of the Sharon group. In fact at the beginning of 1949, James Watt felt he had to leave North Battleford as a result of what he described as 'teaching, revelation and practice' that was departing from the Scripture, specifically 'an extreme position on the manifestations of the Sons of God . . .'.[30] However, as the 1950s went by, the doctrine of the 'manifestations of the Sons of God' was carried to ever-increasing extremes by, for example, Bill Britton.

Britton was an Assemblies of God pastor who embraced the Latter Rain movement in 1949 and became one of its aggressive advocates. His teaching focus was very much upon the Manifest Sons of God and the Man Child company of Revelation 12 theories. He believed that the Man Child company represented the end-times overcoming-church and was quite scathing that any who did not receive this revelation were doomed as belonging to 'Babylon'. To become part of this overcoming-church one needed to become a 'son' which involved a process of maturing in character, in spiritual gifts and in ministry. This led to immortality as one became a 'manifested son'. He wrote many pamphlets and sent out a regular newsletter *Voice of the Watchman* from his headquarters in Springfield, Missouri. Through these publications Britton influenced many in the Pentecostal and charismatic movements for over thirty years with his promises of a victorious, perfect church on earth. In a booklet titled *The Branch*, he writes

> All mankind and all creation is on tiptoe, waiting to see right here on earth the manifestation or the revealing of the sons of God – a church without spot or wrinkle. We will see a perfect church on earth. Can we live for ever? The subject of immortality has disturbed the heart of man for many ages, but only in Christ is this realm of life possible. Fountain of youth, vitamins, water baptism and all other gimmicks to obtain immortality can only fail. He came and overcame, he alone could open the book of life. He alone has immortality, but as joint heirs with him this is our inheritance. This mortal [body] must put on immortality and this corruptible [body] must put on incorruption. We must go after it. We must press towards the mark, defeating the enemy, putting down every spirit that would deter us. This earth must have a witness of this goal being reached. God will put his people on exhibit. People who cannot die, cannot age and against whom no disease can have effect.[31]

Many found the seduction of believing such powerful and attractive promises more than they could resist.

By the time the 1950s ended and the 1960s began, the Manifest Sons of God movement, which had taken in many hundreds of churches and thousands of Christians in America particularly, began to be hit by a number of scandals of one sort or another. The result of this was that many of its adherents simply stopped actively teaching and sharing their beliefs and went underground. However, most of them did not forsake what they believed and many people who were part of both the Latter Rain movement and the Manifest Sons of God movement surfaced years later in the charismatic renewal movement. They had not changed their beliefs and their teaching but brought them lock, stock and barrel, into the charismatic movement.

INFILTRATING THE CHARISMATIC MOVEMENT

Richard M. Riss who wrote what may be described as the definitive history of the Latter Rain movement, and whose research I have used as a primary source, records that 'various beliefs and practices of the Latter Rain found their way into the charismatic renewal, including spiritual singing and dancing, praise, the foundational ministries of Ephesians 4:11, the laying on of hands, tabernacle teaching, the Feast of Tabernacles, and the foundational truths of Hebrews 6:1–2. In addition, elements of various eschatological views of the Latter Rain movement were adopted by many charismatics throughout the world. He then lists nineteen ministries in the United States which flourished in the charismatic renewal and openly espoused Latter Rain teaching.

Although the Latter Rain movement may have started as a sincere desire to see God move in revival and it would be wrong to say that, amongst all that went on, God did not touch people's lives deeply, it and the Manifest Sons of God movement were characterised by considerable spiritual excesses. This included experience-orientated theology based upon a false interpretation of Scripture, an over-emphasis on the gifts of the Spirit – especially prophecy and 'words of knowledge' which were used in directive and manipulative ways both in the lives of individuals and churches – authoritarianism, a 'signs and wonders' gospel and over-realised eschatology. Also an elevation of particular men (i.e. God's new apostles and prophets) to positions of great power and influence amongst God's people, and division and schism in the mainline denominations and sects leading to the setting up of independent churches.

Of course, not everyone in these movements believed everything to the same extent but undoubtedly everyone was to some degree party to these excesses. It is, therefore, very sobering to reflect in retrospect twenty-five years on that since many Latter Rain and Manifest Sons of God adherents automatically signed up for the charismatic renewal movement, variations of these aberrancies became part of charismatic doctrine and practice from quite early on.

For example the Restoration stream within the British charismatic church has been founded on the principle of its leaders being the apostles and prophets 'anointed and appointed' to carry the church forward to its victorious destiny of the end-times. This was the root cause behind the tragedy of 'Shepherding/Discipleship' which decreed that no church fellowship moved without the direction having been indicated by its 'prophet' and no individual believer made any decision regarding how to live his life without the agreement of the church 'apostle' or his designated subordinate.

THE KANSAS CITY PROPHETS

Indeed, by the end of the 1980s, the charismatic renewal movement had become so used to so much extra-biblical experience and, as has been pointed out in the previous chapter, had become focused on the fulfilment of so many eschatological promises, that it was possible for thousands of British charismatic Christians, and their leaders, to be so affected and influenced by the 'prophetic movement' as epitomised by Paul Cain and the 'prophets' from the Kansas City Fellowship in the United States. This movement came to prominence in America as the result of first a sermon and then a published report by Ernest Gruen, a Kansas City pastor, criticising the way in which the leadership of the Fellowship were seeking to take control of the spiritual life of the city. The situation was further promoted by the fact that John Wimber and the Vineyard churches decided to take the Kansas City prophetic movement under their wing and assume responsibility for its future behaviour. The basic complaints being made against the Kansas City Fellowship were the use of directive prophecy to control the lives of believers and take over other fellowships, the use of 'new prophetic revelation' to determine doctrine and practice, and the promotion of an elite group of apostles and prophets centred on themselves. Part of the accusation regarding their 'new' doctrines was that it was simply a return to the old Latter Rain/Manifest Sons of God tenets.[32]

A feature of John Wimber's strategy, with regard to taking on responsibility for the Kansas City prophets and their senior pastor Mike Bickle, was to send in a team of his senior leaders including Dr Jack Deere, a former Professor at Dallas Theological Seminary and now the Vineyard's chief theologian. They examined all the complaints of biblical malpractice being made by Ernest Gruen and published a report acknowledging certain errors which in retrospect to a large degree simply papered over the cracks and allowed the Kansas City Fellowship to continue virtually undisturbed under the Vineyard aegis. The errors which were acknowledged and by implication would not recur included 'the attempt by some prophetic ministers to establish doctrine or practice by revelation alone, apart from biblical support', 'the use of prophetic gifting for controlling purposes', 'using types and allegories to establish doctrine', and 'using jargon that reflects the teaching of groups that we do not wish to be identified with'. This last confession referred specifically to the accusation of promoting the Latter Rain and Manifest Sons of God doctrines. However it must be said that irrespective of how sincerely these errors were acknowledged initially, subsequent events showed that little attempt was made to learn the necessary lessons, especially with regard to the use of establishing doctrine by revelation and the continued teaching of Latter Rain and Manifest Sons teachings.

Paul Cain

The decision by John Wimber and the Vineyard churches to support the ministry of the Kansas City prophets was undoubtedly the result of the link-up which they had made with Paul Cain. Cain had an early history not unlike that of William Branham. Born in 1929, he had been aware of supernatural power guiding his life from its earliest days and had experienced what he believed to be direct communications with the Lord through audible messages whilst still a small boy. He became part of the Pentecostal healing movement which arose in North America in the 1940s and 1950s, led by William Branham, Oral Roberts and others, and began an itinerant ministry as a healing evangelist in his early teens. According to Paul Cain's own testimony he was much encouraged in his ministry by Branham who allegedly saw in him a similar kind of 'anointing' to his own. It is said that there was a particular bond between William Branham and the young Paul Cain, that they frequently ministered together and that Cain would often stand in for Branham at meetings which he was unable to take, although for some unknown reason Cain's association in ministry with Branham has been vehemently denied by the Branham family. However Cain's healing and evangelism ministry was undoubtedly marked by the same kind of 'revelation knowledge' of people and their personal circumstances that had characterised Branham's but by the early 1960s, disillusioned by the 'stardom' status accorded to him and his contemporaries and the general lack of integrity in the ministry, he withdrew from public life and lived as a virtual recluse until he went and met the Kansas City prophets in early 1987.

He believed that the Lord was re-commissioning him for ministry with the special purpose of restoring the prophetic ministry to the church worldwide and that to that end he needed a public platform. His strategy was to be that of taking a prophetic message to every significant evangelical leader in the United States. The leader who responded by accepting him and his message would be the one whom God had chosen to give a platform for his ministry. In 1988, Paul Cain felt he should contact John Wimber and following a visit from Cain, Wimber decided that the Lord was calling him to be the leader who should give Cain his platform.

Paul Cain has consistently denied that he subscribes, or ever has subscribed, to the Manifest Sons of God movement. However, although there is no reason to believe that he was ever a card-carrying member of the movement, his 'prophetic' preaching has clearly promoted the ideas of immortality for overcoming believers here on earth in these end-times and he uses the same spiritual jargon as the Manifest

Sons of God exponents. This comes over in a very specific way in, for example, his teaching on 'Joel's Army'.[33] This teaching, based on the destructive army mentioned in Joel chapter 2, was claimed to be the result of revelation which he had received at the age of nineteen when he had a visitation from the 'Angel of the Lord, and he was standing in his majesty like a warrior and he had a bright shining sword and he pointed up to a billboard like that, and on the sign it said, "Joel's Army in training".' Cain had not understood and had asked, 'Lord, what does this mean?' He had from then on received divine revelation as to the meaning of the book of Joel for today and on this he based his prophetic message. The basic theme of the teaching is that God is about to raise up out of the church a Joel's army. The purpose of this army is to bring in the restoration of the church and a great end-times revival accompanied by signs and wonders the like of which has never been seen before, not even in the life of the early church. These signs and wonders will be accomplished by the 'new breed', the 'dread champions' whom the Lord will raise up to form this mighty army. The purpose of this army is in fact twofold for not only will it be the vanguard of the great signs and wonders revival but it will be responsible for the purging of the church and the destruction of all those who are unworthy to be part of the Bride. Cain teaches in true Manifest Sons style that

> If you have intimacy with God, they can't kill you, they just can't. There is something about you; you're connected to that vine; you're just so close to Him. Oh, my friends, they can't kill you . . . If you're really in the vine and you're the branch, then the life sap from the Son of the living God keeps you from cancer, keeps you from dying,

> keeps you from death . . . Not only will they not have diseases, they will also not die. They will have the kind of imperishable bodies that are talked about in the 15th chapter of Corinthians . . . This army is invincible. If you have intimacy with God they can't kill you.[34]

Paul Cain was, of course, giving this teaching to the Vineyard churches before the Kansas City Fellowship report acknowledging errors, so it could be assumed that following the publishing of that report no further mention would be made of this kind of teaching. It may be of interest to note that at a meeting between John Wimber, Paul Cain and Mike Bickle with Clifford Hill, I asked John Wimber and Mike Bickle if they could specify which teachings were being referred to in the errors acknowledged by the Kansas City Fellowship. Neither was prepared to answer my questions clearly on this subject. It was therefore perhaps not surprising to find that after the Kansas City report both Jack Deere, the Vineyard theologian who had been given the job of checking and verifying the biblical soundness of their teaching, and John Wimber took up the Joel's Army teaching. Wimber propounded it at the London Docklands Conference in October 1990.

In Deere's version of the Joel's Army teaching he underwrites the divine revelation foundation of the teaching and extends Cain's tenets by an extravagant use of hyperbole. He makes the point over and over again that this Joel's Army will be composed of believers who will outshine in their service anything that God ever accomplished through any of his servants in the past. Deere teaches that, 'This army is unique . . . When this army comes, it's large and it's mighty. It's so mighty that there has never been anything like it before. Not even Moses, not even David, not even Paul. What's going to happen now will transcend what Paul did, what David did, what Moses did, even though Moses parted the Red Sea.' Deere goes on to equate this army with the 144,000 in Revelation 7 who, he says, 'follow the Lamb wherever he goes, and no one can harm that 144,000'. Most extraordinarily, he teaches that 144,000 is a multiple of 12 and that since 12 stands for 'apostolic government' then 144,000 is the 'ultimate in apostolic government'.

In his version of the Joel's Army teaching, as given at the London Docklands Conference, John Wimber is much more cautious in his use of language although he undoubtedly underwrites in principle most of both Cain and Deere's teaching. With regard to the great signs and wonders which this army will perform, Wimber simply says, 'This army is large, powerful, unique, unlike any army that's ever existed before or will again. Even as the Lord started this thing with a bang, (Acts 2) he is going to end it with something so incredible that we'll talk about it throughout eternity. It will be the buzz for ever'. However, on the subject of immortality Wimber does not fully support Cain and Deere and says this army will have the 'kind of anointing . . . his kind of power . . . anyone who wants to harm them must die'.

Bob Jones

The leading prophet in the Kansas City Fellowship in 1990 was Bob Jones and it was his prophetic utterances and revelation-based doctrine and practice that was behind most of the controversy that surrounded them and had occasioned Gruen's outbursts. Jones came from Arkansas and in his young days had been a member of the Baptist Church. His spiritual life had, however, been fairly non-existent and he had engaged in petty crime. Nevertheless, his testimony, like Branham and Cain, is of boyhood and early teen 'angelic visitations' including an out-of-body experience at the age of fifteen when he says he was taken before the throne of God. With the advent of the Korean War, Jones joined the US Marine Corps where he became heavily involved in drunken brawls and gambling. With his life in an obviously downward moral and physical spiral he left the Marine Corps and moved to Oklahoma State where he opened an illegal liquor store – Oklahoma being 'dry' – with considerable financial success. However his life of debauchery brought him to the point of a complete breakdown which not even drugs appeared to alleviate, and he ended up in hospital in Topeka near Kansas City where it appears that following a combination of good psychiatric treatment by a Christian doctor and a number of visitations, both divine and demonic, he was discharged.

Bob Jones then started to attend church and read the Bible again and after a number of further 'visitations' he was converted and baptised in the autumn of 1975. Because of the visions and prophecies which he brought to church leadership he found himself often becoming unpopular and ended up being rejected and unable to fit into normal church life. Eventually in the early 1980s Jones found himself accepted by the Kansas City Fellowship – even though Mike Bickle had originally believed him to be a false prophet – where he began to be valued for his prophetic utterances. These were often bizarre and spiritually extravagant. Jones was very much 'into' seeing both demons and angels on a regular basis and having strange nightly visions and out-of-body experiences. According to both Jones himself and Mike Bickle, 'Bob normally gets five to ten visions a night, maybe sees angels ten to fifteen times a week'.[35] Apparently he had been doing this since 1974 and it does not take much mathematical skill to conclude that these supernatural experiences far outweigh all of those recorded as being given to people in the Scriptures!

He was also very much the initiator of spiritual elitism for the Kansas City Fellowship based on 'prophetic revelation' and it seems that the more bizarre his 'prophetic utterances' the more they were promoted by the leadership. For example, he introduced the concept of an 'elected seed generation'. In this he taught that the children born since 1973 to members of the Kansas City Fellowship were the 'elected seed' who had been especially chosen by Jesus and the angels from 'billions of little round yellow things' floating around in heaven to be the 'end time Omega generation'.[36] These 'little yellow things' were the seed from actual blood lines and they were from the 'best of every blood line there has ever been – Paul, David, Peter, James and John – the best of their seed unto this generation'. This elite group were described as 'the chosen generation of all history' who would 'possess the Spirit without measure'. They were also described as 'the Bride of Christ'; the man child of Revelation 12; the ministry of perfection; the Melchizedek priesthood; the manifested sons of God; Joel's Army; and many other biblical epithets.

Jones taught and Bickle underwrote, as senior pastor of the Kansas City Fellowship, that this 'end time, Omega generation super church' would do '10,000 times the miracles in the book of Acts'. They would also conduct meetings of 'a million or more' where they would 'move their hands and the power of God will go like flashes of lightning, and as they go like this over a million people, if a person is missing an arm . . . it will instantly be created'. Jones claimed that 300,000 of Mike Bickle's generation and their super children would be last days' apostles. Thirty-five apostles from the Kansas City Fellowship would be 'like unto Paul'.

Again, we have never been able to find out whether all of these bizarre prophetic teachings of Bob Jones were included amongst the list of errors. When John Wimber brought the Kansas City prophets to Holy Trinity Church, Brompton in July 1990 there was an embargo put on Bob Jones regarding public teaching and prophecy but he was allowed to minister to leaders behind the scenes.

THE BRITISH CONNECTION

The charismatic church in Britain was of course fully exposed to the Kansas City prophets with all their aberrant 'revelation' teaching and their directive personal prophecy. They were first introduced to this country by way of a book entitled *Some Said It Thundered*, written by Bishop David Pytches and published by Hodder and Stoughton in the spring of 1990. David Pytches had made a visit to Kansas City the previous year and his book was an encouraging and sympathetic account of the history of the Fellowship and its prophets. John Wimber then brought a number of them to meet British charismatic leaders at a series of meetings arranged by Holy Trinity, Brompton where he sought to convince them of the authenticity of their prophetic ministry.

Despite the fact that warnings had been given, specifically by Clifford Hill, that much more time and research needed to be put into verifying the Kansas City Fellowship ministry, the majority of British charismatic leaders happily embraced Cain, Jones and the other prophets as truly spiritually credible. In fact a number of them went so far as to sign a statement endorsing the ministry of the Kansas City prophets as being God-given. It is difficult to understand why so many British charismatic leaders were prepared to underwrite this ministry given the bizarre teachings which lay behind it. It can only be assumed that they saw a need to inject into their churches and fellowships the kind of excitement and promise which this prophetic movement generated. It was obviously exciting to many charismatic Christians to be given a glimpse of super-power and great signs and wonders ministry where a powerful church would rule the world for Jesus. This was a glimpse of the fulfilment of all that had been promised to them by their leaders for the previous twenty years. They even had a glimpse of possible earthly immortality. There may also of course have been a sense that the love and respect in which John Wimber was held by most charismatic leaders in the country simply covered a multitude of sins.

One of the important aspects of the visits which John Wimber and the Kansas City prophets made between July and October 1990 was that they raised the expectation for revival in the United Kingdom. In fact Paul Cain went so far as to prophesy that revival would surely come to Britain in October 1990. It was in the expectation of the fulfilment of this prophecy that the London Dockland Conference was arranged that October and so high was the expectation that revival would come that John Wimber brought his whole family from America so that they could be there on the last night. Sadly no revival appeared which brought disillusionment and discouragement to many in the charismatic church. John Wimber himself undoubtedly returned to the United States a very disappointed man. He subsequently distanced himself from the ministry of Paul Cain and there even appeared to be a waning of his promotion of the whole prophetic ministry. Although Paul Cain was taken under the wing of Dr R. T. Kendall, of Westminster Chapel, he did not again appear to have prophetic influence over leadership in the British charismatic church which also appeared to put the whole question of prophecy on hold.

It needs to be stressed that the foundation for the teaching and prophetic ministry of the Kansas City Fellowship, including Paul Cain, was the tenets of the Latter Rain and Manifest Sons of God movements of the 1940s, 50s, and 60s. Despite the protestations and denials that there was any association with these movements, there has never been formal renunciation of their belief in the classic Latter Rain doctrines of the end-times restoration of the church through specially-chosen apostles and prophets bringing her to perfection and the 'overcomers' to immortality, a great signs and wonders ministry surpassing that of the Acts of the Apostles and a great worldwide revival. Similarly there has never been any statement made by British charismatic leadership as to where they now stand on their signed affidavit of July 1990 on the authenticity of the ministry coming from Kansas City. Consequently many are left in confusion as to what is the truth about the prophetic ministry. The lack of solid biblical teaching and honest examination of these experiential events in many charismatic churches simply adds to the confusion.

A NEW DISGUISE?

At the same time, undoubtedly there are many adherents, especially in the United States, of these movements who, although now part of the charismatic movement, have hung on to their original agendas and rejoiced at whatever progress has been made in fulfilling their visions. Although both Latter Rain and the Manifest Sons of God movements lost their overt credibility by the early 1960s it appears that an underground movement for these beliefs has been sufficiently strong for serious attempts to be made from time to time to hijack the charismatic renewal movement. I would contend that one such attempt was made by the prophetic movement as epitomised in the Kansas City Fellowship. I would also contend that what has been dubbed the Toronto Blessing may also be an attempt by some to resurrect the old Latter Rain and Manifest Sons of God visions.

The foreword to Richard Riss's publication on the Latter Rain movement was written in 1987 by James Watt – the same James Watt who had been part of the Sharon group at North Battleford and had inspired George Warnock to write *The Feast of Tabernacles*. Watt says,

> 'In a sense, the fulfilment of the Feast of Tabernacles came forth with the blowing of trumpets from North Battleford . . . the Church has been in part exposed to the day of atonement. The Harvest, or Booths, is now upon us, and the time of the restitution of all things is about to take place . . . The early and latter rain are about to be poured out in the same month! According to Paul Yonggi Cho of Korea and twenty other prophets, the last great move of the Spirit will originate in Canada, and by seventy Canadian cities will be brought to the 210 nations of the earth before Jesus returns.

Marc DuPont, of the Toronto Airport Vineyard, who is considered to have a prophetic ministry, has reported that the Lord gave him a two-part prophetic vision in May 1992 and June 1993 of a mighty wall of water rising in Toronto and flowing out like a river into the rest of Canada.[37] DuPont believed this to be the start of a revival beginning in Toronto and reaching its climax worldwide between the years 2000 and 2005. DuPont also states that, 'This move of the Spirit in 1994 is not just a charismatic and Pentecostal experience, concerning power or gifting. It is one thing to be clothed with power; it is another to be indwelt with the Person of God'.[38] DuPont does not enlarge on what he means by being 'indwelt with the Person of God' and therefore the question needs to be asked whether he envisages 'this move of God' as being the final fulfilment of Latter Rain and Manifest Sons of God visions. George Warnock was of the opinion that the manifestation of the sons of God which would take place at the fulfilment of the 'Feast of Tabernacles' involved the Lord coming to physically indwell his people on earth. His thesis was that when this happened we would no longer have a Head in heaven and a Body on earth but we would have the one new Perfect Man who would fill both heaven and earth. This would be the fulfilment of the Second Pentecost, the early and latter rain of Joel 2. Warnock also believed that there would be a forty-year wilderness experience for the church from the time of the late 1940s Latter Rain revivals until the Second Pentecost.

Randy Clark, who introduced the 'new move of God' to the Toronto Airport Vineyard has recently said that the Vineyard churches have a 'prophetic foundation' for embracing the Toronto Blessing.[39] He has said,

> We are looking for revelation from God as to what he now wants us to do with our lives and in our cities. The prophetic revelation has already been given as a foundation. This is the beginning of a great revival . . . But it's a funtime, a time of empowerment. There will be ebb and flow, there will be a number of waves. There is a time for an

> initial inflow, an initial outpouring. Then a time when God is maturing us, then a time of persecution, then a major outpouring. This is a low power time right now. Someone in Toronto prophesied: I'm giving you my power now in weakness, but there's more coming.

Clark also tells us that the prophetic foundation of what is happening had been prophesied by the Kansas City prophets over ten years ago. He says that in 1984, Mike Bickle 'in visitations from the Lord, the audible voice of the Lord said "In 10 years I am going to visit my people"'. Later, he says a prophecy was given to the Kansas City Fellowship, now renamed the Metro Vineyard, 'The rain is coming'. He further quotes prophecies from Paul Cain and from John Paul Jackson, another of the original Kansas City prophets, that had been given to them in the 1980s that 1993 and 1994 would witness 'this great outpouring from God'. Clark also quoted Paul Cain as saying that at this time God is giving 'sovereign vessels' who are bringing in 'an outpouring of the Lord which is such that it goes beyond anything anybody alive today has ever seen or ever heard or read in church history'. Bearing in mind the prophetic record of the Kansas City prophets regarding previous revival dates, how should we now evaluate these latest predictions?

Rodney Howard-Browne, a South African from the Faith/Prosperity stream (he was a lecturer at Ray McCauley's Rhema Bible School) and often cited as one of the initiators of the Toronto Blessing, is fond of using the old Latter Rain and Franklin Hall 'Holy Ghost fire' imagery. Here is an example of one of his prophecies concerning the Toronto Blessing given at Kenneth Copeland's church in September 1993.

> This is the day, this is the hour, saith the Lord, that I am moving in this earth . . . This is the day

when I will cause you to step over into the realm of the supernatural. For many a preacher has prophesied of old that there is a move coming. But it is even now and even at the door. For the drops of rain are beginning to fall of the glory of God. Yes, yes, many of you who have sat on the threshold and have said, 'O God when shall it be?' O you shall know that this is the day and this is the hour when you shall step over into that place of my glory. This is the day of the glory of the Lord coming in great power. I am going to break the mould, says the Lord, on many of your lives, and on many of your ministries and the way you have operated in days gone by. Many shall rub their eyes and shall say, 'Is this the person we used to know?' For there is a fire inside him. For this is the day of the fire and the glory of God coming into his church. Rise up this day and be filled afresh with the new wine of the Holy Ghost.

SEARCH THE SCRIPTURES

It can be clearly seen that there are blatant associations in this prophecy with the teachings of Franklin Hall, with the teaching of the Latter Rain movement and with the teachings of the Manifest Sons of God groups. So we seem to have come again full circle to a further attempt to involve the church with these non-biblical doctrines. All of us who are sincere and committed believers, not only in God the Father and God the Son but also in a living Holy Spirit who lives within the church as Jesus promised so that he might 'teach us all things', must rejoice when God moves overtly in the lives of his people. According to the Scriptures God is in the business of blessing us and reviving us and if we seek him we will surely find him. However, questions do need to be asked regarding both the spontaneity and genuineness of much that is happening in the charismatic renewal movement today. How much is there of an agenda that is sweeping many of us along without us really being aware of either its beginning or end. I would seek strongly to counsel that the time may be upon us when it is vital for the ongoing health and growth of the charismatic movement that, like the new believers in Berea, we diligently go back to searching the Scriptures to see if the things we are being told are true (Acts 17:11).

CHAPTER FIVE

THE ROLE OF PROPHECY IN THE DIRECTION OF THE CHARISMATIC MOVEMENT

Prophecy is the revelation of divine truth conveyed to a human being by the Spirit of God. The Bible provides a record of God speaking to people from Genesis to Revelation. The prophet was the one to whom God regularly spoke and he bore the responsibility of declaring the word of God to the people. The office of the prophet was recognised in Israel from the time of Moses whose brother and sister, Aaron and Miriam, heard God say to them,

> 'When a prophet of the LORD is among you,
> I reveal myself to him in visions,
> I speak to him in dreams.
> But this is not true of my servant Moses;
> he is faithful in all my house.
> With him I speak face to face,
> clearly and not in riddles; . . .'
>
> (Num 12:6–8)

Moses himself looked forward to the day when all true believers would be able to hear directly from the Lord, 'I wish that all the LORD's people were prophets and that the LORD would put his Spirit on them!' (Num 11:29).

The prophet Joel said that this would happen in 'the last days'. Concerning those days he prophesied,

> '. . . I will pour out my Spirit on all people.
> Your sons and daughters will prophesy,
> your old men will dream dreams,
> your young men will see visions.
> Even on my servants, both men and women,
> I will pour out my Spirit in those days.'
> (Joel 2:28–29)

The apostle Peter saw the relevance of that prophecy on the Day of Pentecost which he believed heralded the beginning of 'the last days'. In the streets of Jerusalem when he addressed the crowd he quoted Joel, but added the words 'and they will prophesy'. Clearly he did this to emphasise the significance of prophecy, of hearing from God. It is clear from the New Testament record that the purpose of prophecy in the early church was to enable the church to be rightly guided by the Lord in carrying out its mission to fulfil the great commission given to them by Jesus – to go into all the world carrying the good news of salvation to all peoples.

Nowhere in the New Testament is it said that the ability to hear from God would be withdrawn or that God would cease to communicate with his people through the Holy Spirit. There are, however, many warnings in the New Testament concerning false prophets and clear instruction is given about handling prophecy and testing anything that purports to be divine revelation.

Jesus himself gave severe warnings: 'Watch out for

false prophets. They come to you in sheep's clothing, but inwardly they are ferocious wolves. By their fruit you will recognise them' (Matt 7:15–16).

He added the warning that these false prophets would have the ability to exercise supernatural power and 'perform many miracles' in his name, but they would be false prophets not commissioned by the Lord. Those warnings were not given simply for the apostolic age but for generations to come.

Before examining the role of prophecy in directing the development of the charismatic movement it is important to establish biblical principles, to understand the role of the prophet and how to identify the false prophet.

THE ROLE OF THE PROPHET

Throughout the history of ancient Israel God always sent prophets in times of crisis. He did not simply allow judgment to fall upon the people without sending abundant warnings. These warning signs were part of his love and mercy shown to his people. The prophet's task in each generation was to recognise and rightly interpret the signs. As Amos observed, 'Surely the Sovereign LORD does nothing without revealing his plan to his servants the prophets' (Amos 3:7).

It is important to note that God never sent prophets to Israel to announce blessing. He never sent his prophets to herald times of peace and prosperity. It was the false prophets who came with these messages. God raised up true prophets in times of impending disaster to warn the people, to call them to repentance and to return to the Lord their God, that the disaster might be averted. God did not need to send prophets to announce times of blessing because *that was the normal state in which his people should have been living*. But the enjoyment of God's blessing was always conditional upon the faithfulness of his people. When they turned aside to the worship of other gods, or became involved in pacts and treaties with other nations that drew them away from the Lord, or when the lusts and desires of the world turned their hearts away from the paths of righteousness, then God withheld his blessing and things began to go wrong. These were the warning signs picked up by the prophets.

The whole purpose of the prophetic ministry is to bring warnings of danger and of the inevitable consequences of turning away from God. This basic principle of the prophetic ministry is expressed by Jeremiah in his dispute with Hananiah who was foretelling a time of blessing and revival in the fortunes of the nation. Jeremiah said, 'From early times the prophets who preceded you and me have prophesied war, disaster and plague against many countries and great kingdoms. But the prophet who prophesies peace will be recognised as one truly sent by the LORD only if his prediction comes true' (Jer 28:8–9).

This is an important statement which touches the very heart of the prophetic ministry and gives the key to its understanding within the context of the history of Israel. Hananiah's message was delivered with all the authority of the true prophetic word as though it came directly from the mouth of the living God.

> 'This is what the LORD Almighty, the God of Israel, says: "I will break the yoke of the king of Babylon. Within two years I will bring back to this place all the articles of the LORD's house that Nebuchadnezzar king of Babylon removed from here and took to Babylon. I will also bring back to this place Jehoiachin, son of Jehoiakim king of Judah and all the other exiles from Judah who

went to Babylon," declares the LORD, "for I will break the yoke of the king of Babylon." '

(Jer 28:2–4)

This sounded like a true prophecy. It was just what the people wanted to hear and Hananiah's popularity rating must have soared whereas Jeremiah's standing in Jerusalem plunged to a new low. He was shunned as the man of doom and gloom.

There were serious consequences of Hananiah's false prophecy. It not only gave the people false hopes, but it actually turned them away from hearing the true word of God. It became a stumbling-block to their repentance and their turning back to God and coming under his covering and receiving his blessing.

FALSE PROPHECY

False prophecy always does great harm to the people of God. It not only deceives and misleads them, building up false hopes, but it actually becomes a stumbling-block to the Word of God. It deceives the faithful people who trust these prophets and turns their hearts away from God so that they fail to heed what he is saying to them. It was a shattering experience for Jeremiah who saw the inevitable consequences of unfaithfulness and clearly foresaw the destruction of Jerusalem. He loved his nation and he loved the city where he exercised his ministry so he was heartbroken to see the devastating effects of false prophecy, 'My heart is broken within me; all my bones tremble,' he said (Jer 23:9). He went on to plead with the people:

'Do not listen to what the prophets are prophesying to you;
they fill you with false hopes.

They speak visions from their own minds,
not from the mouth of the LORD.'

(Jer 23:16)

Jeremiah heard God saying,

'I did not send these prophets,
yet they have run with their message;
I did not speak to them,
yet they have prophesied.
But if they had stood in my council,
they would have proclaimed my words to my people
and would have turned them from their evil ways
and from their evil deeds.'

(Jer 23:21–22)

Eventually Jeremiah had to face the prophet Hananiah, although several times he had tried to avoid the confrontation. In the end he said to him, 'Listen, Hananiah! The LORD has not sent you, yet you have persuaded this nation to trust in lies.' Jeremiah saw the false prophecy for what it really was, 'You have preached rebellion against the LORD' (Jer 28:15–16).

False prophecy always incites the people to rebellion against the will of God. This was clearly seen by Moses when he taught the people how to discern between the true prophet and the false. He said that the false prophet, 'must be put to death, because he preached rebellion against the LORD your God, who brought you out of Egypt and redeemed you from the land of slavery; he has tried to turn you from the way the LORD your God commanded you to follow' (Deut 13:5).

It was no doubt with this in mind that Jeremiah said that God would remove Hananiah from the face of the earth (Jer 28:16).

He recognised the very serious consequences of

false prophecy which misleads the people and blinds them to the true word of God. The effects of false prophecy are exactly the same today. It is for this reason that we need to distinguish clearly between true guidance from God which enables the church to fulfil the mission of Christ in bringing the Word of God to the world and that which comes from the human imagination or from another spirit. We see today a battle for the truth that bears many similarities to that which was fought in the early church.

Most of the epistles in the New Testament were written to counter false doctrine by establishing the truth and there are numerous warnings from the apostles that anyone teaching a different gospel or deviating from the truth revealed to them by the Lord Jesus was teaching heresy. Paul warned the Corinthians not to accept anyone who preached a different Jesus or a different gospel from the one they had accepted through him (2 Cor 11:3–5) and he warned Timothy, 'What you have heard from me, keep as the pattern of sound teaching, . . . guard it with the help of the Holy Spirit who lives in us' (2 Tim 1:13–14).

At the beginning of the twentieth century a similar warning appeared in one of the earliest prophecies to emerge from the Pentecostal movement. It was given in Azusa Street in 1906,

> In the last days three things will happen in the great Pentecostal movement:
> There will be an over-emphasis on power rather than on righteousness.
> There will be an over-emphasis on praise to a God they no longer pray to.
> There will be an over-emphasis on the gifts of the Spirit, rather than on the Lordship of Christ.

THE CHARISMATIC MOVEMENT

Prophecy was regularly exercised in the Pentecostal movement throughout the first half of the twentieth century. It was given a place of special importance within the Apostolic Churches. The office of the prophet is one of the ministries referred to by Paul in Ephesians 4 and prophecy is also one of the gifts or 'manifestations of the Spirit' in the list given by Paul in 1 Corinthians 12. It is therefore not surprising that prophecy should have featured strongly amongst charismatics both as a ministry and as a spiritual gift exercised by any believer within a local church setting. There are two new factors which have affected the use of prophecy in the charismatic movement and distinguished it from early Pentecostalism. They are:

Lack of organisation

There is a lack of organisation in the charismatic movement which has not only formed a wide variety of independent fellowships with no regulatory body, but has also spread across the denominations. The Pentecostal movement by contrast established denominational structures at a fairly early stage providing accountability for local pastors and a point of reference for the establishment of agreed biblically-based teaching and practice. Within local fellowships individual church members exercised spiritual gifts under pastoral authority.

The charismatic movement has generally lacked these safeguards although that would not be true of all local churches. In many mainline churches touched by the renewal the ministers simply did not know how to handle spiritual gifts. I myself spent four years in theological college but when I was ordained I had received no teaching at all on the spiritual gifts. They were deemed to have ceased at the end of the apostolic age and were therefore irrelevant for today. My experience would be typical of all ministers up until the 1970s – and indeed for many beyond that date!

Additionally, many individual believers who experienced the baptism of the Holy Spirit were in churches where the minister did not recognise, or actually suppressed, the spiritual gifts. They therefore formed small house fellowships and made up their own rules. As has already been noted in earlier chapters, some of these fellowships broke away from mainline churches or from Brethren Assemblies and formed the independent charismatic streams we have today.

Latter Rain influence

The second major factor influencing the exercise of prophecy in the charismatic movement was the Latter Rain Revival. This has been dealt with in some length in Chapter Four so we will not be dealing in detail with those prophecies here.

It is, however, essential to note that the movement itself began in response to a prophecy, and prophecy became one of the major distinguishing marks of the movement. Indeed, the original prophecy which gave birth to the movement said that people would be brought into the Latter Rain blessing 'by prophecy and the laying on of hands'. This was immediately seen to be fulfilled when five students at the Sharon Bible School came forward to receive the blessing after their names had been revealed by prophecy.

One of the main areas of controversy between the leaders of the Sharon group and the Pentecostal denominations was the manner in which the former used prophecy, especially in relation to the place of apostles and prophets in the present-day church. The Latter Rain leaders taught that revival and the restoration of the church was being effected through 'end-times' apostles and prophets specially ordained by God for the purpose. The prophets provided the revelation from God as to what the church should both believe and do and the apostles provided the authority structure to put things into practice. This thinking has of course become quite prevalent in the charismatic movement over the last twenty-five years.

However, the leaders of the Pentecostal denominations (particularly the Assemblies of God) soon charged the Latter Rain leadership with seeking to exercise authority over people and churches by the use of directive prophecy. They were also concerned about what they saw as 'novices' prophesying in these circumstances and accordingly rejected both as being unbiblical.

It was a strong belief in both the Latter Rain and Manifest Sons of God movements that prophetic revelation, giving new understandings and interpretations of Scripture, was one of the marks of the last days restoration of the church. This view has had an ongoing pervasive influence in the charismatic movement and may well account for the fact that often prophecy is accepted when it has little scriptural basis, being viewed as acceptable on the grounds of it being 'prophetic revelation'. Although most charismatics would deny this, in practice, they have treated contemporary prophetic revelations as the direct word of God on a par with Scripture.

These views are not of course new to 'end-times' teachings. Variations of them were responsible for the emergence of strange and heretical doctrines in earlier generations; for example, the heresy of the Free Spirit which broke out in one form or another throughout Europe during the Middle Ages. This heresy which always involved prophetic revelation sought to offer people the blessing of receiving the Holy Spirit in such measure that they became like

Jesus and that, like him, they could become divine. It was seen in Tanchelm and his followers in twelfth-century Flanders, in the Franciscan Spirituals who followed the prophecies of Joachim of Fiore and in the Amaurians of thirteenth-century France.

TWO STRANDS OF PROPHECY

An examination of prophecies coming out of the charismatic movement reveals two strands. On the one hand there have been prophecies giving warnings of difficult days and testing times. Secondly, by contrast, there have been prophecies with promises of revival and restoration predicting good times and days of prosperity. We look first at those prophesying testing times and the shaking of the nations.

Warnings

Some of the earliest prophecies giving warning of difficult days ahead were given in the main-line churches. The following, for example, was given in 1975 at an international conference of Catholic Charismatic Renewal Groups.

> 'Because I love you, I want to show you what I am doing in the world today. I want to prepare you for what is to come. Days of darkness are coming on the world, days of tribulation . . . Buildings that are now standing will not be standing. Supports that are there for my people will not be there. I want you to be prepared, my people, to know only me and to cleave to me and to have me in a deeper way than ever before. I will lead you into the desert. . . . I will strip you of everything that you are depending on now, so you depend just on me.
>
> 'A time of darkness is coming on the world, but

a time of glory is coming for my church, a time of glory is coming for my people. I will pour out on you all the gifts of my Spirit. I will prepare you for spiritual combat. I will prepare you for a time of evangelism that the world has never seen. . . . And when you have nothing but me, you will have everything: lands, fields, homes, and brothers and sisters, and love and joy and peace more than ever before. Be ready, my people, I want to prepare you. . . .'[1]

Another prophecy, even more specific in its warnings of economical and social upheaval came from Catholic charismatic renewal groups at a national meeting in the USA in January 1976.

'Son of man, do you see that city going bankrupt? Are you willing to see all of your cities going bankrupt? Are you willing to see the bankruptcy of the whole economic system you rely upon now, so that all money is worthless and cannot support you?

'Son of man, do you see the crime and lawlessness in your city streets, and towns, and institutions? Are you willing to see no law, no order, no protection for you except the protection which I myself will give you?

'Son of man, do you see the country which you love? Are you willing to see no country, no country to call your own except those I give you as my body?

'Son of man, do you see those churches you can go to so easily now? Are you ready to see them with bars across their doors? Are you ready to depend only on me and not on all the institutions of schools and parishes that you are working so hard to foster?

'Son of man, I call you to be ready for that.

> 'The structures are falling and changing. It is not for you to know the details now, but do not rely on them as you have been. I want you to trust one another, to build an interdependence that is based on my Spirit. This is an absolute necessity for those who would base their lives on me and not on the structures of a pagan world.'[2]

There were many prophecies of a similar vein in the mid 1970s. One which was addressed specifically to church leaders also came from the USA. It was given at an interdenominational charismatic renewal conference which was attended by leaders of most of the mainline churches including Pentecostals, but with the exception of the Assemblies of God. The prophecy was a strong word calling for repentance.

> The Lord has a word to speak to the leaders of all the Christian churches. If you are a bishop or a superintendent or a supervisor or an overseer or the head of a Christian movement or organization, this word is for you. The Lord says:
>
> 'You are all guilty in my eyes for the condition of my people, who are weak and divided and unprepared. I have set you in office over them, and you have not fulfilled that office as I would have it fulfilled, because you have not been the servants I would have called you to be.
>
> 'This is a hard word, but I want you to hear it. You have not come to me and made important in your lives and in your efforts those things which were most important to me; but instead you chose to put other things first. You have tolerated division among yourselves and grown used to it. You have not repented for it or fasted for it or sought me to bring it to an end. You have tolerated it, and you have increased it.
>
> 'And you have not been my servants first of all

in every case, but you have served other people ahead of me, and you have served your organization ahead of me. But I am God, and you are my servants. Why are you not serving me first of all?

'I know your hearts, and I know that many of you love me, and I have compassion on you, for I have placed you in a very hard place. But I have placed you there, and I call you to account for it. Now humble yourselves before me and come to me repentant, in fasting, mourning, and weeping for the condition of my people . . .'[3]

Another prophecy coming from within the mainline churches in the early days of the renewal movement was delivered in Canterbury Cathedral at an international Anglican conference on spiritual renewal in 1978. The message not only referred to things that were wrong within the church but also gave an uplifting message of God's desire to restore and renew his church.

'Within this mighty edifice – the stones cry out.
The stones beneath your feet cry out;
The stones beside you cry to heaven,
And these that soar to heaven cry out too.
The stones cry out – of glory and of shame.

'They cry out – of time when cloud and fire
From God on high came down
And filled this place.
And some saw that and some saw not.
Some had their lives transformed;
Some went on and plodded on the way
And saw no vision of night or day,
To take them in the new and living way
Which called them on.

'These stones cry out – have always cried
In thousand years of love, grace, power

And of the great consuming fire of God.
But I say to thee –
That I have greater things to make
Than this great building.
I have a living work to do
With stones that live –
In infinite and gracious detail
In the quarry of my heart.

'I look upon the stones that I have made,
And they are wayward stones.
From their surface chisel oft has glanced aside
And that which I did purpose has been marred;
And yet I stoop again with broken tool
To take the stone that I have made
And work again upon that stone,
That it may be as I have
Long desired it should be. . . .

'And let these stones cry out
Of what the living stones must be. . . .
That you may truly
High exalt the Saviour's name.'[4]

Ten years later also in Canterbury Cathedral, Patricia Higton gave a more specific warning that the desire for unity and good relationships with people of other faiths was leading the church dangerously towards multi-faith worship.

'I have been speaking to you of unity. And yes, you are beginning to understand that you must reflect my divine nature in its harmony. But I would say to you I am a God of creativity. The unity which I long to see amongst my children will be a diamond with many facets. Each facet will reflect something of my revelation but is of little worth unless part of the whole. So there must be a glad recognition that you belong

> together and need each other. But again I would warn you, my children, that my enemy is seeking to bring about a unity which is not based on my word. It will appear to have as its goal the peace of this world, but it is not centred on the cross of my Son.
>
> 'I am warning you of these things for I would not have any of you deceived by wandering down the path of acceptance, leading to toleration of any form of worship which does not uphold my name and my word. The end of that path is that many will one day worship a christ who is not my Son. *The very stones of this building will witness this terrible thing, unless my church repents.*'[5]

This warning went unheeded and the prophecy was fulfilled the following year when a 'Festival of Faith and the Environment' was held at Canterbury Cathedral. People of all faiths and philosophies were invited to participate and were encouraged to join a 'pilgrimage' walk from temples and shrines of other faiths culminating in a multi-faith celebration in the Cathedral. The multi-faith festival brought protests from evangelicals of all denominations. The protest within the C of E was led by Tony Higton, a leading Anglican charismatic, Director of ABWON (Action for Biblical Witness to Our Nation) founded in 1984. An open letter to the leadership of the Church of England opposing multi-faith worship was signed by over 2,000 clergy which sent shock waves through the hierarchy, and the activities of Cathedral Deans who were arranging a number of multi-faith activities came to an abrupt stop. This is an indication of the power of prophetic witness to influence church policy even in days when scant respect is paid to biblical correctness.

Five years prior to the Canterbury festival a new

magazine, *Prophecy Today* was launched in London by the ministry which I lead. From the beginning it has carried an uncompromising biblically-based message. Its editorial policy statement reads:

> It is published with the intention of conveying the word of God for our times to the people of God, and through them to the nations of the world. We define prophecy as the forthtelling of the word of God. This was the task of the prophets in ancient Israel. It is the task of the church today . . . Christ wants his church to be a prophetic people proclaiming his word to his world. It was for this reason that the Holy Spirit was given to the New Testament community of believers. We also believe that the present world situation is so serious that the very existence of mankind is under threat. In all the nations a spirit of violence and disorder appears to have been loosed that is disturbing family life, disrupting the community, overthrowing moral and social stability and threatening to lead to world-wide destruction. We believe that the root problems facing mankind are not simply economic, social or political, but spiritual, and that the gospel is the only answer. We note that in times of crisis in ancient Israel God used the prophets to alert people to danger and to correct their ways, . . . so today we believe God is longing to use his church in this prophetic role in the world. The most urgent need for the nations is not to hear the opinions of men, but to hear the word of God. It is as a contribution towards the prophetic task that *Prophecy Today* is published.[6]

By the early 1990s *Prophecy Today* had reached a circulation in excess of 16,000 – the largest circulation of a Christian bi-monthly magazine in the UK.

With each copy being read by an average of three persons this means that *Prophecy Today* is read by approximately 50,000 in the evangelical/charismatic churches. Typical of the warning note it has sounded is the following prophecy:

> 'The nation is sick and heading for massive disaster, but I hold my church primarily responsible for the moral and spiritual life of this nation. You are the watchmen of the nation and you have not been faithful upon the walls of the cities to discern the onslaught of the enemy or to blow the trumpet to warn the people of danger, so the enemy has been allowed to come in like a flood and pervade the land. The land has been polluted by the shedding of innocent blood, by violence and pornography, by adultery and sodomy, by corruption and injustice, by greed and avarice, by oppression and unrighteousness, by lies and deceit, by witchcraft and idolatry and by a lack of compassion for the poor and powerless.
>
> 'In the face of all this evil and corruption your voice is still not heard in the nation. The prophetic declaration of the word of God is not heard upon the lips of the leaders of the church. It is for this reason that the church languishes, its numbers are in decline, its finances are unhealthy and there is disunity, discord and a lack of vision.
>
> 'Now is the time to repent. Now is the time to recognise your faithlessness and the way you have strayed from the paths of righteousness and failed to uphold my word in the nation. If you will now repent publicly of your own sinfulness and declare my word within the church and in the sight of the whole nation, the people will respond. If you refuse to hear this word and harden your

hearts against me, you will bring upon yourselves terrible consequences as the days darken across the nations.'[7]

Several prophecies that were influential in the charismatic movement were given at an international conference in Israel in April 1986. These were the first to give forewarning of the shaking of the nations which would be accompanied by a worldwide harvest as the church continued to expand rapidly in many nations. The shaking of the nations would be through both political and economic upheaval. One of the prophecies said that the great shaking was about to begin with the Soviet Union. Three weeks later the Chernobyl nuclear power station erupted which began the shaking of the USSR and led to its eventual demise. The following is a small part of one of the prophecies.

It referred specifically to the downfall of Gorbachev and the collapse of the Communist empire: 'I, only I, can overcome this evil regime. But through the prayers of my people I will break the power of this man. For this reason you should pray for your enemies. I will send a famine. It will bring the Kremlin to their knees and make them open to my word.'[8]

Four years later this prophecy was fulfilled in the breakup of the Soviet Union and the Warsaw Pact countries of Eastern Europe. It was the famine caused by the Chernobyl meltdown which began the whole process.

Promises of revival and blessing

We look now at prophecies which contrast strangely with the warnings. By far the most popular prophecies among charismatics have been those promising renewal and speaking of days when great power and prosperity would be enjoyed by the Lord's people. These prophecies actually pre-date the charismatic movement and began in the Latter Rain Revival movement in North America. Reference has already been made to these prophecies in Chapter Four. It is relevant here to note their persistence over a period of more than fifty years. Concepts which have no biblical foundation, some of which were banned as heretical in the 1940s have reappeared time after time in the charismatic movement. They have been popularised by charismatic speakers and uncritically accepted.

A prophecy by David Minor which was given to an assembly of the Lutheran Church in the USA had a wide circulation among charismatics reaching many countries. It conveyed a message with a promise of revival preceded by a time of cleansing and purification of the church. These were described as 'winds'. It is a long prophecy but it is reproduced here in full because of its influence in the charismatic movement.

> TURN YOUR FACE INTO THE WIND
> 'The Spirit of God would say to you that the Wind of the Holy Spirit is blowing through the land. The church, however, is incapable of fully recognizing this Wind. Just as your nation has given names to its hurricanes, so I have put My Name on this Wind. This Wind shall be named "Holiness Unto the Lord".
>
> 'Because of a lack of understanding, some of My people will try to find shelter from the Wind, but in so doing they shall miss My work. For this Wind has been sent to blow through every institution that has been raised in My Name. Those institutions that have substituted their name for Mine, they shall fall by the impact of My Wind. Those institutions shall fall like cardboard shacks in a gale. Ministries that have not walked in uprightness before Me shall be broken and fall.
>
> 'For this reason man will be tempted to brand

this as the work of Satan, but do not be misled. This is My Wind. I cannot tolerate My Church in its present form, nor will I tolerate it. Ministries and organizations will shake and fall in the face of this Wind, and even though some will seek to hide from that Wind, they shall not escape. It shall blow against your lives and all around you will appear crumbling. And so it shall.

'But never forget this is My Wind, saith the Lord, with tornado force it will come and appear to leave devastation, but the Word of the Lord comes and says, "Turn your face into the Wind and let it blow." For only that which is not of Me shall be devastated. You must see this as necessary.

'Be not dismayed. For after this, My Wind shall blow again. Have you not read how My Breath blew on the valley of dry bones? So it shall breathe on you. This wind will come in equal force as the first Wind. This Wind too will have a name. It shall be called "The Kingdom of God".

'It shall bring My government and order. Along with that it shall bring My power. The supernatural shall come in that Wind. The world will laugh at you because of the devastation of that first Wind, but they will laugh no more. For this Wind will come with force and power that will produce the miraculous among My people and the fear of God shall fall on the nation.

'My people will be willing in the day of My power, saith the Lord. In my first Wind that is upon you now, I will blow out pride, lust, greed, competition and jealousy, and you will feel devastated. But haven't you read, "Blessed are the poor in spirit, for theirs is the Kingdom of Heaven"? So out of your poverty of spirit I will establish My Kingdom. Have you not read, "The Kingdom of

> God is in the Holy Ghost?" So by My Spirit, My Kingdom will be established and made manifest.
>
> 'Know this also, there will be those who shall seek to hide from this present Wind and they will try to flow with the second Wind. But again, they will be blown away by it. Only those who have turned their faces into the present Wind shall be allowed to be propelled by the second Wind.
>
> 'You have longed for revival and a return of the miraculous and the supernatural. You and your generation shall see it, but it shall only come by My process, saith the Lord.
>
> 'The church of this nation cannot contain My power in its present form. But as it turns to the Wind of the Holiness of God, it shall be purged and changed to contain My glory. This is judgment that has begun at the house of God, but it is not the end. When the second Wind has come and brought in My harvest, then shall the end come.'[9]

This prophecy became influential in the charismatic movement as much for its emphasis upon 'holiness' as for the reinforcing of the expectation of supernatural power. But the concept of 'holiness' it conveyed was not biblical. The Hebrew understanding of holiness was of separation from the world. Hence the prophets could speak of the 'wholly otherness' of God. The temple vessels and priestly garments were 'set aside' from common use for the exclusive service of God.

But this popular charismatic concept of holiness does not speak of a people 'set aside' from the world for the exclusive service of God – a people who have renounced the values and ways of the world. It concentrates upon personal morality; the elementary things which all people of goodwill who accept the Ten Commandments as the basic rule of life should be following. There is nothing special about turning away from 'pride, lust, greed, competition and jealousy' which the prophecy says will cause the Lord's people to feel devastated!

In testing this prophecy we should ask, why should this make us feel devastated? But the prophecy was never subjected to biblical testing – it was simply uncritically accepted because it sounded good and made people feel good. So it was passed around charismatic churches across the world. Nobody queried the phrase 'Have you not read, "The Kingdom of God is in the Holy Ghost?" ' the answer to which has to be NO! It's certainly not in the Bible! Yet it is subtly used here to introduce a promise of 'a return of the miraculous and the supernatural. You and your generation shall see it'.

This promise is certainly not in the Bible. Nevertheless promises like this appeal strongly to western Christians who long for power and prestige in a world where they feel powerless and lacking in social acceptance.

Another prophecy which had considerable influence in the charismatic movement was published as a small booklet entitled 'The Harvest' by Rick Joiner.[10] In this he predicted a time of worldwide revival and great spiritual awakening. This was fully in line with the expectations and hopes of charismatics. It was a popular word that was eagerly received and passed on from one to another. It helped to reinforce the belief that a great and glorious, supernaturally-endowed church was about to be raised up by God. This belief was picked up and passed on by many charismatic leaders who incorporated it into their teaching so that it became part of the accepted body of doctrine in the charismatic movement.

Undoubtedly the prophecies which have had the greatest influence in directing the development of the charismatic movement have been those coming from the Vineyard/KCF ministry. The Vineyard group of churches was founded by John Wimber in 1981 and in 1989 the Kansas City Fellowship of six churches was incorporated. Their major emphasis was upon prophetic revelation. Wimber recalls that in 1987 he himself was at a low ebb in his spiritual life. He told his congregation that he hadn't heard from God for about two years.[11] Nothing was going right in his ministry. David Watson, with whom he had become firm friends, had died of cancer despite Wimber's confidence that he would be healed. Up to that time he had been saying that they were seeing a considerable proportion of healings amongst those prayed for, including the healing of cancer. He has since confessed that that was not true and they actually saw very few healings. Wimber's cup of bitterness was compounded in 1987 by the discovery of adultery and immorality among his leaders. He struggled to rectify these things during the next year and then he records, 'on December 5th 1988 Paul Cain visited me in Anaheim. Paul was living in Dallas, Texas, at that time, and he had a proven, mature prophetic ministry – on a level of which I had never heard before . . .'[12]

Paul Cain had been out of ministry for thirty years since the death of Branham and his days as a Latter Rain Revivalist preacher. He says that God told him to attach himself to a man with an established ministry in order to promote his teaching about an end-time 'new breed' of men anointed with supernatural power. He could hardly have chosen a more appropriate moment to approach Wimber whose ministry appeared to be on the wane and who was in a highly vulnerable condition. Cain also accurately predicted a minor earthquake in California which convinced Wimber that God had sent him.

Paul came with reassuring words that God was

> with us. He said, 'God has told me to tell you in the Vineyard, grace, grace.' He said that if we repented God would spare us from judgment for our sins. Further, I was admonished to no longer tolerate low standards and loose living in the Vineyard, and to discipline and raise up a people of purity and holiness. My role, he said, would be significantly altered – more authoritative and directive. . . . Paul Cain (and others) also introduced a new dimension of ministry and God's working to the Vineyard. . . . We have produced few people with a prophetic ministry . . . quite honestly, I didn't take prophecy too seriously. All that has now changed. During this past year I have had to look at prophecy *seriously* for perhaps the first time in my life.[13]

Paul Cain was introduced by Wimber as a prophet of extraordinary spiritual power and insight. He was presented to the British churches as the herald of a new breed who would be the end-time people of God possessing extraordinary spiritual power. In the write-up prior to his public meetings in Britain it was reported,

> Today it isn't unusual for Paul to call out twenty or thirty people by name in meetings and to know the most intimate details of their lives (family relationships, birthdays, secrets of their hearts, prayers, where they live) and then bring prophetic direction regarding repentance, forgiveness, calling, gifting, and ministry.
>
> However, the most satisfying aspect of Paul Cain's ministry isn't his remarkable prophetic insight into people's lives, although naming people and knowing intimate details of their lives does catch one's attention. More significant is his clarion call – by word and example – to live holy

> lives that are submitted to God, and thus join the new breed of men and women whom God is raising up in the 1990s.[14]

This promise of a 'new breed' was central to Cain's teaching. There can be no doubt that Wimber saw Cain as a divine messenger to give revelationary confirmation and support to his own teaching of 'power evangelism', power healing and power for signs and wonders and miracles. Speaking on Wimber's platform in Anaheim in 1989 Cain said that there was going to be a worldwide spiritual awakening and the gospel was going to reach every part of the earth. It's going to,

> reach every cavern, every cave, every foxhole, every land, every tongue, every nation, . . . God is going to reach them with the supernatural, with the power evangelism that John Wimber so eloquently speaks about. It is the power evangelism that's going to do it. . . .[15]
>
> I tell you we're in a crisis stage right now where the church is going to be forced to pray and forced to believe for the prophetic ministry because that's our only salvation. If God doesn't raise up apostles and prophets and power evangelists and pastors and teachers, then we've had it because the church is going to fade into oblivion. . . .[16]

This 'prophecy' is based upon Latter Rain teaching and the expectation that the restoration of the offices of apostle and prophet would be the key to raising a glorious end-time church to rule the world. Cain continued:

> God has reserved a day after due process and after preparation. God is going to raise up a people out of a people and they're going to be a bunch of nobodies from nowhere. They may not

> have a lot of degrees and they may not have a lot of clout and they may not have a lot of PR, they may not have a great vocabulary, they may not even be able to do any more than groan in the Spirit, but if that's all they do, it's going to be power. It's going to be powerful and it's going to accomplish more than all the beautiful words of oratory in the world . . . the Lord is doing his new things in these last days. The gospel of the kingdom is not just the word, it is the word and power. The word will do you no good.[17]

It is hard to imagine what Cain meant by the phrase 'the word will do you no good' as he did not elaborate it, but when such phrases slip out it indicates something basically wrong with the preacher's attitude to Scripture. Cain's prediction that ordinary people with little education and no special status were going to be given supernatural power was a highly popular prophecy received with great acclamation.

A significant element in the Vineyard/KCF ministry team which was developed in the late 1980s was the way in which the prophets confirmed one another's prophecies and added additional concepts which became incorporated into the body of teaching being given through the ministry. Bob Jones, for example, confirmed Cain's teaching on 'the new breed' and stated that this elite company of believers would eventually achieve divinity. He saw them,

> progressively going on in this righteousness until you take on the very divine nature of Christ himself and you begin to see Christ in the church. Christ won't come for the church until you see Christ in the church. Papa planted Jesus, he sowed him down here in this earth to have a whole nation of brothers and sisters that looked just like Jesus and he will have it. My daddy's big

> enough to have his way and he's going to have him a nation of priests and kings. That's what his heart's desire is to have him a nation of sons and daughters that will talk to him just like his son did. His son was an alpha son, your children are the omega sons and daughters.[18]

Jones believed that the generation of children born since 1973 would form the final generation of believers whom God was preparing as the Bride of Christ to take control of the world and present the kingdom to Christ on his return. He continued, 'I do believe what he's beginning to do is a restoration of his very nature down here. Your children will come behind you and they'll start on your level of righteousness and holiness and they'll take off from there.'[19]

This, of course, is complete fantasy and a denial of the teaching of Jesus who said, 'no one can see the kingdom of God unless he is born again' (John 3:3).

Our children cannot inherit our righteousness however much they may benefit from our love, our teaching, and our personal example. Jones went on to say that he had 'a literal visitation from the Lord' and that Jesus told him a new version of Psalm 12:1, that it should read 'Help, Lord, release the champions, the dread champions'. In the Bible, Psalm 12:1 reads 'Help, Lord, for the godly are no more; the faithful have vanished from among men'. Jones's version[20] is completely different and has no other authority except his claim to have had a personal visitation and personal revelation from God. On the strength of that vision he built a whole doctrine which has been accepted by John Wimber and incorporated into the Vineyard teaching. This became clear from Wimber's use of the concept.

In the leaflet advertising the October 1990 meetings there was a personal message from John Wimber who wrote, 'God has given us a vision to see the body of Christ move from being an inactive audience to a Spirit-filled army'.[21]

This sounds wholly good and highly attractive to ministers who have seen very little growth in their churches, and to church members who long to break out from the cocoon of traditionalism that has characterised the church in Britain for much of the twentieth century. But Wimber continued, 'In our opinion God is about to unloose a powerful outpouring of the Holy Spirit of an unprecedented magnitude . . . He is looking for individuals who will be "dread champions" for his cause'.[22]

The significance of this phrase would have been lost on most of those who hurried to return their booking forms and £60 registration fee (excluding accommodation and food). The phrase 'dread champions' was part of the teaching being given by Wimber, Cain and the Kansas City prophets. It was linked with their teaching about 'a new breed' whom God was going to raise in the last generation before the Second Coming of Christ to evangelise the world and subdue the nations.

Peter Fenwick, in Chapter Three, has referred to one of the foundational teachings of the Restorationist movement being that evangelism would no longer be necessary because God was going to do it as a sovereign act. The respected and renewed church would be so attractive that unbelievers would flock to it. This teaching was at the heart of the Wimber message in 1990. But by this time he had added a significant new dimension to 'restorationist' teaching. Wimber believed that signs and wonders performed by a elect company of leaders through a mighty impartation of supernatural power would sweep unbelievers into the kingdom. In essence, this belief lay at the heart of his teaching on 'power evangelism'.

A few months before they came to Britain that year Paul Cain had been teaching at Anaheim with John Wimber setting out his beliefs. He said that God was bringing to birth a new breed of Christians who would actually be the incarnate word of God and through them the gospel of the Kingdom would be proclaimed, not simply by their words but by their lives. Cain said: 'God's strange act is going to bring a new order of things and bring a new breed in and bring a transformation.'[23]

Amid much clapping, shouting, whistling and cheering he told the crowd,

> There's going to be something in the wave of power and evangelism in these last days. Little children are going to lay their darling little hands on the sick and heal multitudes . . . We are going to be just like the Lord in that respect. They're going to say, 'Here comes that dreadful, fearful army of champions. Here comes those with a word of knowledge, the word of wisdom, the working of miracles, with a healing ministry, with the power to heal the sick and raise the dead, with the power to know what's going on behind the Iron Curtain.' You're going to really be a fearful group before this thing's all over with and I am resting in that.[24]

It is noticeable that Cain had picked up Jones's phrase about an 'army of champions'. This is another example of the prophets confirming each other's words. This is a highly dangerous practice which was roundly condemned by Jeremiah:

> 'Is not my word like fire,' declares the LORD, 'and like a hammer that breaks a rock in pieces? Therefore,' declares the LORD, 'I am against the prophets who steal from one another words sup-

> posedly from me. Yes,' declares the LORD, 'I am against the prophets who wag their own tongues and yet declare, "The LORD declares".'
>
> (Jer 23: 29–31)

In ancient Israel the law required that the testimony of one witness should be confirmed by that of at least one other. If several prophets came declaring the same message it was regarded as divine confirmation. In Jeremiah's day the false prophets were picking up popular prophecies from each other saying that God would not allow Jerusalem to fall to the Babylonians, that the Egyptians would come to their aid, and that no harm would come to the people. This encouraged them to continue living in the kind of idolatry and immorality described in Jeremiah 7:1–12 and it closed their minds to the warnings God was sending through the true prophets.

Bob Jones, Paul Cain, John Paul-Jackson, Jim Goll, Mike Bickle and Jack Deere, (the Kansas City Fellowship School of Prophets) all confirmed each other's prophecies, adding bits out of their own imaginations. These all sounded good to the people so they were readily believed, even though they were contrary to Scripture. But the Word of God does not change: 'How long will this continue in the hearts of these lying prophets, who prophesy the delusions of their own minds?' (Jer 23:26).

Cain's prophecies were highly popular and the crowd got even more excited when he told them that God was about to give them this supernatural power which would transform their lives.

> God is saying 'Arise and shine, for your light is come, behold the darkness will cover the earth and deep darkness, but the Lord will raise you up, the Lord will rise upon you and the nations will come to your light. You're going to shine,

> shine, shine! You're going to be the light of day and the light of life! . . . God's going to have a whole company of people that are going to be like that and then the world will see the light and they are going to come to it, they are going to see it, all nations will come to your light and that's the way we are going to get world evangelisation.'[25]

This teaching, which so excited the people, was utterly false, but John Wimber endorsed it so the people accepted it. They probably did not know the Bible well enough to know that it is Jesus who is the Light of Life and the words from Isaiah 60:1, 'Arise, shine, for your light has come,' are part of a prophecy about the coming of Messiah. Surely God will not share his glory with anyone else and nations will come to *his* light not to ours. It is surely a wicked deception to say 'the nations will come to *your* light'! It is also interesting to see how Cain used prophecy to confirm the Latter Rain teaching that world evangelisation would result from the supernatural power which was going to be given to believers. This teaching was central to Wimber's message.

In the same speech Paul Cain prophesied that the new breed would possess power to overcome the enemies of the gospel and strike terror into them, 'There's going to be an awesome, reverential fear and respect for the church because the church is going to regain her power, lose her restrictions, lose her weakness . . . you're going to be called upon by presidents and kings of nations, heads of state.'[26]

He then went on to say that believers would be given the power to strike dead those who opposed them, as happened to Ananias and Sapphira. He said that he knew two men who possessed this power, they were William Branham and Mordecai Hamm. He said, 'If I had a hero, I think it would be William Branham or Mordecai Hamm.' He continued,

> God is going to have his army and they are going to be a fearful bunch and they are going to go to every place on the face of the earth. All we have to do is see two people so anointed, two people here, two people there, two people over yonder and they will go forth and take that part of China, that part of Africa, that part of that island, or that whole island, or this nation or that nation, for one can set a thousand to flight and two can set ten thousand to flight.[27]

It is amazing what flights of fantasy people will absorb and actually believe if their respected leaders tell them it is true. This is what has been happening in the charismatic movement, yet we scornfully dismissed the Hindu 'milk miracle' in September 1995. *The Times* reported that throughout Britain Hindus 'gripped by a devotional frenzy' queued up at the local shrines to offer spoonfuls of milk to their gods. 'It began with rumours on Thursday that the elephant-headed Gamesh idol in a New Delhi suburb had drunk half a cup of milk and within 24 hours millions of Hindus around the world seemed to have heard of the "signal from the gods" (*The Times* 23.9.95).

Some of the things we ask people to believe at charismatic celebrations are almost as unbelievable as the Hindu milk miracle. In the same speech as that reported above amidst much cheering and clapping Paul Cain promised,

> You just wait until God does this strange act. Well, they'll fall all over you getting to God. All we have to do is seize what we are talking about tonight and they'll fall all over you getting to God!

> You are going to employ the tools of the trade after the impartation comes.[28]

He went on to say that John Wimber was going to give that impartation: 'When brother John Wimber stands here and gives that impartation, you're going to see more signs and wonders.'[29]

This teaching on 'impartation' is another doctrine which comes from the Latter Rain movement. Franklin Hall taught that he was given by God the power to impart immortality. He was giving this teaching in the early days of the Latter Rain movement in the 1940s but as recently as 1988, forty years later, he was still giving the same teaching. He said at that time that at the moment he only had the power to give partial immortality from the feet up to the knees but gradually this would extend to the whole body.

This teaching on impartation has been picked up by others in the charismatic movement. For example, in the March 1995 newsletter sent out from Kingdom Faith Ministries by Colin Urquhart he writes,

> Dear friends, REVIVAL IS HERE! Praise God! The revival breakthrough has come to us at Kingdom Faith, by the grace of God. This month's tape tells you of the anointing that has caused this to happen. It is a word of personal testimony of what happened when Hector Gimenez was told by God to impart to me the same anointing that was on his own life.[30]

This teaching on impartation is contrary to Scripture. As David Noakes shows in Chapter Six, the teaching of Haggai 2 shows that we are able to pass on corruption but not blessing. Blessing comes down directly from God. We can of course pray for God to bestow blessing upon someone, but we cannot *impart* that blessing ourselves. That authority is not given to us as human beings.

This is just one of the many aberrations and errant teachings that have got into the charismatic movement through false prophecy which then becomes incorporated into doctrine and forms part of a body of false teaching such as that which is being currently passed around in the charismatic movement.

Perhaps the charismatic stream that has been most influenced by Latter Rain and Manifest Sons of God is 'Classical Restorationism' which picked up many of the elements of 'revelation' teaching, including the restoration of the offices of apostle and prophet, shepherding, discipleship, authoritarianism, the attainment of godhead and immortalisation. These prophecies have been summarised by Albert Dager. This shows the extent to which teachings which have no biblical foundation have become accepted in the charismatic movement through the influence of Restorationism.

Summary of Latter Rain prophecies

1. In the latter days, the offices of apostle and prophet will be restored.
2. The prophets will call the Church to holiness and rejection of the world's influences found in the denominational churches. True sonship with God will come through stages of perfection: servant, friend, son, and ultimately, godhood itself;
3. The apostles will rule the Church through the establishment of independent churches, unaffiliated with the corrupt denominations. The exception would be denominational churches that leave their covering and join the movement;
4. Through signs and wonders wrought by the apostles and prophets, a worldwide revival will break out, and a majority of the world will be won to

Christ. The signs and wonders will include blessings upon those whom the apostles and prophets bless, and curses upon those whom they curse;

5. The revival will come as the result of the Church defeating demonic spirits through prayer, fasting, and spiritual warfare conducted through intense worship and praise, and by rebuking demonic powers and territorial spirits. The restoration of worship and praise is known as the restoration of the Tabernacle of David, and includes dancing, singing, and exuberant praise in tongues;

6. Those who achieve a certain degree of holiness under the direction of the apostles and prophets will overcome all enemies, including death, and will become immortal. They will complete the conquest of the nations before Christ returns. The conquering will be done as Joel's army – an army of immortal beings – bringing judgment upon the ungodly and all who will not accept the authority of the apostles and prophets;

7. Some believe that the second coming of Jesus is in and through the Church: the Church will become Christ on earth and rule the nations with a rod of iron. Others believe that after the Church has taken dominion over the nations (or a significant portion of the nations), the Church, glorious and triumphant, will call Jesus back to earth and hand the nations over to him. Those who hold the latter view are willing to overlook the heresy of the former in the interest of unity with the purposes of realizing their goal of conquest.[31]

CONCLUSION

The charismatic movement has witnessed an enormous number of prophecies over the last twenty-five or more years. These have been given in small house groups, church congregations, at celebration events and in many publications of all kinds. They have come from believers exercising the gift of prophecy, or individuals giving prophetic messages to each other, or from well-known leaders and preachers at large gatherings.

Many of these prophecies have simply been received and forgotten, but others have had great influence. They have been passed from one to another, recorded on tape and published in magazines and books.

The prophecies which have exerted the most influence have not been warnings but have been the popular words promising 'revival' and great spiritual power. This influence can be measured objectively through the amount of publicity given and the number of leaders who quote them. Another objective measure is to note the concepts which come from contemporary prophetic 'relevation' and have become incorporated into doctrine such as the 'Joel's Army', 'dread champions' or 'new breed' teachings.

The charismatic movement has absorbed all these and many more. They have been highly influential in giving direction to the development of the movement and especially in the formation of charismatic doctrine. The most popular belief to have come from this source is the expectation of a great spiritual revival and the emergence of a glorious, victorious, supernaturally empowered church. So widespread is this belief that there can be few charismatics who know that it has absolutely no biblical foundation. It comes from Latter Rain prophecy and is actually contrary to Scripture. Yet it has been enthusiastically adopted by countless preachers and passed on to their people as though it were the Word of God. This is a measure of the deception in the charismatic movement because even if the people do not know the Bible well enough to test doctrine and to recognise heresy, surely the preachers should be able to do so! Or is it a case of 'all we like sheep have gone astray'? If one well-known leader endorses it, all the other minor leaders accept it, and so the people are misled.

When the promises fail to be fulfilled some new, exciting and entertaining diversion is readily embraced with inadequate testing. It was the great expectations engendered by Latter Rain prophecies popularised by the Wimber team in 1990 which prepared the way in Britain for the ready acceptance given to the bizarre antics of the Toronto phenomenon.

There is, however, something even more serious than engaging in strange behaviour and believing it to be inspired by the Holy Spirit. The most serious consequence of accepting false prophecy and believing false teaching is that it can cause blindness to the true Word of God. It can also act as a major diversion from the purpose of God for his people at a particular time. If God is warning about an impending difficult time and the people are deceived into thinking good times are coming they will be unprepared when the storm breaks.

The many prophecies of warning have been largely ignored in the charismatic movement, whereas the popular prophecies of good times have been received with joy. It is a sobering thought that in ancient Israel God never sent prophets to announce times of prosperity. It was the false prophets who came with these messages which were always popular with the people, while the true prophets were stoned. Hundreds of generations later, we are prone to the same errors of judgment. The most popular sins are the sins of the fathers.

CHAPTER SIX

A PERSONAL AND BIBLICAL PERSPECTIVE OF RENEWAL

The history of Israel tells us that again and again the Hebrew nation, despite the Law, despite the warnings of the prophets, walked in ways of their own choosing and not in the ways of God. They chose the way of the flesh, the way of self-will and disobedience, in preference to the will of their God; they chose to compromise and to make an accommodation with the spirit of the world in which they lived, to worship not only the God of Israel but also the false gods of the surrounding gentile nations, and to walk in the ways of the world from which God had called them to be separate. The final outcome we know: disaster and exile, from which the promised return is only now taking place.

The church likewise in every era of her history has faced the same basic problems and the same moral choice. The pressures and the subtle attractions of the world-system which surrounds God's people confront us daily with the need to distinguish the ways of God from the ways of the world, and to make the choice to walk according to the Spirit and not according to the flesh; to walk in the will of God to the exclusion of the clamouring demands of the flesh in the form of self-will and self-indulgence. The climate of the present age in which we live is, however, perhaps the hardest to withstand which the church has yet encountered.

THE SPIRIT OF THE AGE

In the society of the western nations, the spirit of this age is one which seeks and demands the instant and the spectacular. The world's heroes are those who display outward charisma; their often morally bankrupt character is regarded as irrelevant. Instant success in the forum of materialism or of entertainment guarantees a man wealth and the status of a celebrity. The achievements of electronic circuitry and other scientific advances have made commonplace instantaneous results in many fields of daily activity, and have brought intolerance of all that depends on plodding, painstaking labour to achieve its results. In this disposable society enduring results are not necessary; all is ephemeral, tomorrow we will throw away yesterday's wonder and get the new and better one which will by then be being offered.

Such attitudes, and the spiritual atmosphere which they engender, bring only death to the church which begins to accept and to embrace them. No longer is it seen as acceptable that 'through faith and patience [we] inherit' the promise of God (Heb 6:12); we must have it all now. No longer is the discipline of waiting upon God and waiting for God regarded as relevant, but instead we want to be like the world. We crave for instant and spectacular results. The spirit of the age has deluded us into thinking that the church ought to be experiencing heaven on earth, here and now, forgetting the plain teaching of Scripture that this cannot be until the return of Jesus (1 Pet 1:3–7). We are encouraged to live in expectation that all problems should be speedily swept away, that financial hardship and ill-health should be eliminated; to believe in a magic-carpet type of Christianity in which we may rub the Aladdin's lamp and summon forth the genie who will do all our bidding for our comfort and prosperity – forgetting the teaching of Scripture that 'We must go through many hardships to enter the kingdom of God' (Acts 14:22).

As Clifford Hill states in Chapter Two, it was into an age in which this sort of spirit was coming increasingly to hold sway that the charismatic renewal movement was born in the years leading up to 1960. The fear of the Lord was being replaced by contempt and disregard for the moral law contained in his Word, which was coming to be seen as an unnecessary restriction upon a society which had never had it so good.

The beginning of the charismatic renewal movement in Britain can be dated to the conferences convened by Arthur Willis and David Lillie, the first taking place in 1958. This new move of the Holy Spirit had the potential to revitalise and revolutionise the church, bringing about whole-hearted repentance, a return to the ways of God as revealed in his Word, and a thoroughgoing and radical revolution in church life bringing back a quality of Christian corporate living scarcely seen since the first century; or alternatively it could fall under the influence of the spirit of the age and the ways of the world in which it found itself.

Sadly, the evidence tells us that the latter tendency has largely prevailed. In few places has the self-sacrificing quality of life of the early church been re-established, and there has been nothing which could be seen as having the character of revival. In the church as a whole, numbers have continued to decline, biblical standards of morality have been abandoned wholesale, and the British nation has turned farther and farther away from God, while the church has embraced the spirit of the world and has been sapped by it of spiritual vision and vitality.

To watch the unfolding of the history of the charismatic renewal movement has been for me a matter of great personal sadness. Having spent the early years following my conversion under the influence of sound evangelical doctrine, a foundation for which I shall ever be grateful to God, I received the baptism in Holy Spirit in 1967 as a result of a sovereign action of the Lord – on a train travelling to Brighton to transact some business! Following this unlikely-seeming event, I was introduced to the supernatural manifestations of the Holy Spirit, all of which I believe wholeheartedly are not only valid today, but will become of increasing importance to the church in the days which are to come – days not of comfort, but of pressure; not of dominion, but of conflict and persecution; not of ease, but of the refiner's fire; days of turmoil and upheaval when God will be shaking all that can be shaken, both among the nations of the world and also in the professing church.

DAYS OF PREPARATION

Believing this to be so, I perceive the times in which we are living as being, for the church, days of preparation. I have come to understand God's purposes in renewing the activity of the Holy Spirit among us as being to strengthen the church for the days to come, re-establishing our foundations upon Scripture, teaching us again how to live corporately as the early church did, renewing the closeness and intimacy of our relationship with himself, and empowering us to be fearless and unshakeable witnesses to the truth of his Word.

Possibly the most important single purpose of God in this visitation of his Spirit was to renew our understanding, and hence our outworking, of the corporate life of the Body of Christ. The church has for generations been crippled in her functioning by our western-style individualistic way of life, which has been such a feature of Protestant Christianity. Vital though the Reformation was, it brought with it also this disadvantage. Rooted in the Renaissance, with its rediscovery of Greek classical thought, philosophy and literature, the Reformation brought into the Protestant Reformed churches a Hellenistic view of life which is profoundly different at many points from that of the Hebrew.

To the Hebrew minds of those who formed the early church, corporateness was instinctive; it was a concept built from the very beginning into the structure of the Hebrew nation descended from Jacob. Hence to them, the concept of the church as a corporate entity presented no great problem of adjustment in their thinking – it was easy for them to understand its structure in the light of concepts such as that of the Body of Christ, or the corporate Temple made of living stones. They were able to understand their oneness in Christ in a way which the Greek-thinking mind does not easily grasp.

I believe we need urgently to let God renew our western way of thinking in this whole matter, for it is only in the context of the commitment to one another which is established by a corporate understanding of the church as the Body of the Lord Jesus that we shall be able to stand firm and glorify him when the days of testing are upon us. It is significant that the chief purposes of the fivefold ministry appointments of

Ephesians 4, and of the manifestations of the Holy Spirit specified in 1 Corinthians chapters 12 to 14, are to build up the corporate Body of Christ in such a way as to bring strength and unity and to equip us as members of that Body to be able to carry out the purposes of Jesus, the Head.

So far, more than thirty-five years after those earliest beginnings of the charismatic renewal movement, this has really not happened. There are a few notable exceptions, but most of the church has made little or no progress towards the corporate unity in Christ which brings forth the quality of Body-life of which we read in the early chapters of the book of Acts.

ISHMAEL OR ISAAC

Some twenty years ago, during a time of heart-searching and of questioning over the developments of the newly-introduced doctrines of discipling and shepherding, which had operated to destroy a beautiful work which God had been doing among a group of deeply-committed Christians, I sought God for enlightenment and found that I was being drawn in the Scriptures to the account in Genesis of the activity of Abraham in bringing forth first Ishmael and then Isaac.

I began to realise that embedded in that story was a great spiritual principle. Both Ishmael and Isaac were born as a result of Abraham's faith in believing God's promise that from his offspring would come blessing to the nations of the earth. The initiative in the whole matter came from God; of that there was no doubt. Abraham's response was one of faith. Yet the end result brought not only fulfilment and joy; but also tragedy and sorrow, heartbreak and strife, and an enmity which continues to cause conflict in the Middle East to this very day between the descendants of Ishmael and those of Isaac.

Why did this mixed result emerge from Abraham's belief in a promise of God which was intended only for blessing and not for evil? The reason lies in Abraham's failure to understand that the Lord who had made the promise had also already chosen the method of its outworking. When we receive revelation from God of his intentions and purposes, there are two possible ways of responding: the way of the flesh, which seeks to work out God's purpose as quickly as possible in the ways of human wisdom and ability, or the way of the spirit, which hears from God but then waits for him to reveal further his chosen time and means of fulfilling his intentions.

Abraham, then, was faced with the option of these two different types of response to the revelation of God's purpose. God was going to do what he had said, and he was going to do it in his own time and in his own way; but how was Abraham going to co-operate? Would he 'by faith and patience inherit the promise'? Would he display the maturity which he later showed when he was willing to sacrifice Isaac on Mount Moriah, believing that God would still fulfil his Word even if humanly that had been made impossible? Would he be willing to wait in faith for a further fourteen years until God's appointed time for the birth of Isaac, the promised heir?

Abraham did not wait. How much strife and suffering could have been avoided if only he had! Instead, he and Sarah applied their human wisdom and understanding and decided how, since Sarah was barren, they could accomplish the purposes of God and bring his promise to fruition. They decided how best to help God out in the doing of his own work.

In spiritual terms, they were deciding how the flesh

could achieve the Spirit's work. But this is by definition impossible: nothing which is of the flesh, of man's self-will, can ever please God or accomplish his will. What Abraham and Sarah were planning was an unholy mixture of the revealed will of God with the activities of the flesh in seeking to bring the revelation into being.

At Sarah's suggestion, Abraham acted on human initiative and sought, successfully, to produce offspring from the body of Hagar, Sarah's maidservant. This offspring was, of course, Ishmael, who was to be the root from which sprang the Arab nations; but he was not the heir whom God had promised.

Hagar was Egyptian. We must not miss the significance of this, for in Scripture Egypt is a type of the world-system out of which the Christian has been saved. Abraham, acting in the flesh, had employed the ways which the world could offer in seeking to carry out God's purpose – but it was to no avail. Ishmael was not the fulfilment of God's promise. When the fulfilment, Isaac, was manifested fourteen years later, he would come as the result of a miraculous sovereign work of the Spirit of God. God would not use the methods of either fleshly wisdom and endeavour, nor would the ways of the world be involved in any way. It is always so with God.

He would visit Abraham and Sarah in their extreme old age and by the power of his Spirit, having waited until humanly it was beyond possibility, he would bring forth Isaac from their marital union.

From this account, contained in Genesis chapters 15–18 and 21, I began to understand that God was speaking of a parallel which was and is taking place within the charismatic renewal movement. Ishmael stands for that which men's wisdom and activity can bring forth in the flesh by way of fulfilling God's purpose. Isaac, however, represents the true fulfilment of the Lord's revealed intentions, a work which his Spirit alone can accomplish, for which men must wait for God to act at his own time and in his own way.

The principle embodied in the account of how first Abraham produced Ishmael and then God brought forth Isaac remains true today. God asks us to co-operate with him in the outworking of his purpose through our exercise of faith, patience and humble obedience, refusing to fall into the trap of supplementing or even replacing God's work by our own human efforts. The alternative course is that of human endeavour, prompted by a degree of awareness of what it is that God purposes to do, but with insufficient knowledge of his chosen method and too much haste to await his further revelation.

The first way of responding brings blessing and life. The second has within it from the beginning the seeds of its own demise because that which is born of human striving and wisdom is of no value in accomplishing the purposes of God. To seek to organise God's work for him leads eventually to failure, disillusionment and confusion, and finally even to deception and error.

I believe that for nearly twenty years, God has been indicating that within the charismatically-renewed churches we have in various different ways been producing Ishmael and not Isaac. God gave in the late 1950s to David Lillie and Arthur Wallis a vision of how the fresh visitation of the Holy Spirit was intended to bring about a return of the church to a structure and a way of life which we find revealed in the pages of the New Testament, particularly in the books of Acts and Ephesians. It was of a corporate body of God's people functioning together in such a way that through them by the powerful working of the Holy Spirit would be brought glory to God in the church (Eph 3:21) and a revelation to the world of the true character of the Lord Jesus; a body of people separated as the early church was, neither relying upon the world nor compromising with its ways. That was the vision which was communicated to the key leaders who attended those early conferences.

Sadly, what we now see is so far from the purity of vision as to be almost unrecognisable, and the reason is that the ways of the world have infiltrated deeply into the charismatic renewal movement. We have been invaded in a variety of ways by the spirit of the age in which we live.

THE WORLD IN THE CHURCH

We can now see within the church the equivalent of the world's superstars, the hero on a pedestal supported and followed by his admirers. In some cases, the gifted man in leadership has been exalted in the minds of his followers to a point of infallibility, which brings both him and them into great danger. Within the last year, a mature Christian man with leadership responsibilities said to me: 'David, I simply cannot believe that X (a prominent charismatic leader) could possibly get anything wrong'. I could only respond that in that case, he had effectively elevated the man to the status of God, bringing both of them into great peril. We have brought into being the phenomenon of the Christian guru.

During the last twenty years we have seen emerge another characteristic of the spirit of the age – the desire to create large-scale enterprises, to build church empires. This is the ecclesiastical equivalent of the multi-national conglomerate commercial organisation, ruled through a hierarchical authority structure with exalted executives directing operations and visiting outposts of their empires from their central headquarters. It has much of the world's ways about it, but little of the biblical revelation of the structure of the church or of the servant-leadership of which Jesus speaks in Matthew 20:25–28 and 23:1–12.

The world's delight in spectacular entertainment has infected the church with the love of the big show on the public platform. Twenty-five years ago we would see lines of people quietly waiting to receive the laying-on of hands so that the Holy Spirit would show the compassion of God in bringing gifts of healings. Now, however, we have progressed to the point where we expect that in place of the ministry of the Word and prayer, men will perform as magicians to cause others to fall to the floor, for no good reason, but simply as a demonstration of power. This is far removed from the activities of the Jesus revealed in the Gospels, who disdained to exercise power for wrong purposes. He was consistently unwilling to perform signs and wonders to impress, but only in order to demonstrate the compassion of his Father to the sick and the needy and as confirmation of the truth of the Word which he spoke. Many meetings now, however, are not for the purposes by which he was motivated, but for those of worldly display, financial gain and the elevation of the ministries of men.

The materialism of the western world and its 'get rich quick' philosophy has entered the church in the form of the prosperity gospel. By 'naming and claiming' we seek to oblige a penny-in-the-slot god to deliver the goods which a hedonistic philosophy desires. Paul would have found it very hard to believe in such teaching in the midst of his impoverishments, imprisonments and shipwrecks! Yet the church wants to be like the world, luxuriating in a form of self-indulgent religion. 'To the law and to the testimony' cries Isaiah 8:20. What does the Word of God say of this? 'Keep falsehood and lies far from me; give me neither poverty nor riches, but give me only my daily bread. Otherwise, I may have too much and disown you and say, "Who is the LORD?" Or I may become poor and steal, and so dishonour the name of my God' (Prov 30:8–9). The scripture explains clearly the wisdom which underlies the teaching of Jesus that we are to ask simply for our 'daily bread'.

HOW HAS THE WORLD GAINED ACCESS?

What has made possible this wholesale invasion of the church by the thinking and the ways of the world? Most of those who have introduced these ways are men who originally started well as ministers of the Word. What has ensnared us?

The largest factor leading us to embrace the world and its methods is exactly that which led Abraham into the trap of his liaison with Hagar – the operation of the uncrucified flesh, the inherent drive towards self-gratification rather than to what is pleasing to God. The permanent conflict within us between spirit and flesh, so plainly spelt out in Romans 8 and Galatians 5, always poses one stark question: whose will is going to be carried out, that of God or that of self?

The attributes of the self-centred, self-gratifying flesh will always drive us away from the Lord and into the embrace of the world. As with Abraham and Sarah, the flesh causes us to think that we know best and can manage God's business quite well for him. This pride, however, for that is what it is, opens the way to the desire for wealth, for fame and for the praises of men; and to the urge to exercise within the church, not godly authority, but worldly domination and control over the lives of others.

As a result, leaders unwittingly usurp the place of

Jesus as Head of the Body, just as Jezebel usurped the authority of her husband King Ahab. Instead of gifted leaders being used by the Holy Spirit in his primary purpose of building up the Body of Christ, they often became the agents of causing the people of God to become crushed and ineffective under a religious tyranny, unable to grow and mature as the Lord would desire. A further effect of overbearing leadership, and one which is potentially of immense and far-reaching danger, is that all discernment of the source of spiritual activity becomes the prerogative of leaders and the rest of the people have often no alternative but to stifle the witness of the Holy Spirit within them. We shall return to this topic later.

DOCTRINAL ERROR

Pride, and its accompanying desire for power and dominion, all too easily opens the door to false doctrine. Taken together with the vital ingredient of the deep root of anti-Semitism, the largely unadmitted and unrepented sin of the gentile church through so many generations, pride has opened the way for the doctrines of Dominion theology and for the false concepts of Restorationism and Reconstructionism.

The rejection of the clear and unambiguous teaching of Scripture concerning the continuing part which the nation of Israel has to play in the purposes of God throws away a vital key to a biblical understanding of the significance of the times in which we live. It leads to error and confusion in eschatology; to deny that God will fulfil all his Word concerning Israel in the closing days of this age is to throw away, as it were, the hub of the eschatological wheel into which all ancillary doctrine fits like spokes. Discard Israel from the equation and there is no clear understanding of how the rest can fit together. We cannot understand how or when the coming Day of the Lord will affect the church or the world unless we first understand how that event will affect Judah and Jerusalem.

The concepts of Restorationist thinking can only be sustained alongside a theology which maintains that God has replaced Israel with the church; and to hold that theological position involves the assertion that God has broken his Word of assurance to the Hebrew nation, particularly with regard to their restoration to the land given as an everlasting covenant to the descendants of Abraham, Isaac and Jacob (Ps 105:8–11). The God whom we know as the Father of our Lord Jesus Christ is not, however, one who breaks his Word of covenant, for to do so would be to deny his very character. He will undoubtedly fulfil to the uttermost all his Word concerning the descendants of Jacob.

Restorationist teaching and the accompanying 'Dominion' or 'Kingdom Now' theology depends, however, upon an interpretation of Scripture which denies that God will fulfil his Word concerning Israel. Such an interpretation is utterly false. The basic concept of Restorationism stems from an erroneous understanding of Acts 3:21. This verse is interpreted to mean that God will restore the church to a glorious condition in the world before the return of Christ. However, the same verse goes on to define this restoration as being that which God has promised to do through the Hebrew prophets. Of what, then, did they predict the restoration? They prophesied concerning the restoration of the Davidic kingdom (Amos 9:11–15) and all that accompanies it, which will be restored by the action of the Messiah at his return. No 'restoration of all things' prior to the Second Advent is predicted by the prophets of Israel.

Why should this error of understanding matter so

greatly? Clearly it must matter for the fundamental reason that any distortion or error in interpretation falsifies the Word of truth and misleads those who are wrongly taught. In the times into which we have now entered, however, it has an additional peril for those who have been misled by it. False doctrine gives rise to false prophecy, and false prophecy leads to confusion and disillusionment because of the failure of its expected fulfilment.

In that part – and it is a very considerable part – of the charismatically-renewed church which has espoused Restorationist thinking and Dominion theology, there has been a consistent strain of prophecy predicting glory and dominion, power and rulership for the church before the return of Christ. Triumphalism has been a dominant feature. It is very appealing – it appealed strongly to me when I was first hearing it more than twenty years ago – but its appeal, unfortunately, is to the flesh in us. Who would not prefer to be the head, rather than the tail?

The problem, however, is that neither the basic doctrine nor this prophetic theme are true; they are both deceptive, for neither accords with the revelation of the Word of God concerning the last days in which we are now living. These are days, not of increasing light, but of increasingly great spiritual darkness on the nations of the earth (Is 60:2), which will intensify until he who is the Light of the World returns. Along with this darkness will come the false light of the increasing power and extent of New Age religion, leading ultimately to the worship of Lucifer.

THE DANGERS OF DECEPTION

The greatest peril to the church, and one which will increase in danger as time progresses, will be that of deception. This is the teaching of Jesus and the Apostles in the New Testament. Satan will assume increasingly his two principal roles (Rev 12:9) of both dragon and serpent – persecutor and deceiver – and he will employ both means in causing many to fall away (Matt 24:9–13). Deception, however, is his preferred method, for by it he can cause men unwittingly to serve his purposes. We are warned in 2 Corinthians 11:14–15 that Satan masquerades as an angel of light, and his ministers as ministers of righteousness. If the church is not alert and discerning, we will surely be deceived, for he will prove too subtle for us unless we have open ears to hear and to heed the warnings which the Holy Spirit gives against deception whenever it arises, as more and more frequently it will surely do.

COUNTERFEIT SPIRITUAL MANIFESTATIONS

Although deception is no new weapon against the church – much of the writing in the New Testament Epistles had the exposure of deception as its purpose – nevertheless of all the signs of the imminence of the Second Coming and the end of the present age, the increase of deception is the sign of which we are given the most consistent warning. When the disciples asked this very question of Jesus concerning the signs of the end of the age, he began his reply with the words: 'Watch out that no-one deceives you' (Matt 24:4). He immediately warns them of the emergence of false Christs (v 5) who 'will deceive many', and in verse 11 of false prophets who 'will appear and deceive many people'. There is further warning in verses 23 and 24 concerning the appearance of false Christs and false prophets who 'will appear and perform great signs and miracles to deceive even the elect – if that were possible.'

Jesus is warning of false men who will seek to validate their deceptive claims by performing great signs and wonders. They will manifest great spiritual power and bring about amazing activity – yet nevertheless, they are not sent by God. Satan is a master of counterfeit spiritual phenomena, as he had demonstrated when Pharaoh's magicians by their occult powers duplicated Moses' action in turning his staff into a snake, and then also duplicated the phenomena of the first two plagues which Moses pronounced upon Egypt (Exod 7:6–8:15). The source of their power was entirely different, but the results appeared identical. It was not until the third plague, of gnats, that God did not permit the magicians to succeed, at which point they recognised and declared to Pharaoh that the plague must be from God; their own source of power was no longer operating.

What a warning we should draw from such an account in Scripture. The outward evidence was identical, but the origin of their power was occult. If we look simply at outward appearances, impressive as they may be, we are candidates for deception. It is for this reason that the New Testament gives us so much clear warning concerning counterfeit spiritual activity. This is not so that we should become afraid of the genuine and reject all spiritual phenomena out of hand; rather the reverse, for the more the deceptions come against us, the more we shall need the genuine powerful activity of the Holy Spirit in order that we may discern and counter it. Our need is not to reject spiritual manifestations, but to become increasingly alert and practised in distinguishing the source of the power behind them (Heb 5:14).

Paul gives clear warning in 2 Thessalonians 2 concerning the coming of the Day of the Lord and the return of Jesus. He declares that first a figure known as the man of lawlessness (or man of sin, the personification of the spirit of Satan, sometimes called the antichrist) will appear. This person will be overthrown and destroyed at the return of the Lord Jesus; but before that, warns Paul in verses 9–11, he will display by the activity and power of Satan 'all kinds of counterfeit miracles, signs and wonders' and 'every sort of evil that deceives those who are perishing. They perish because they refused to love the truth and so be saved. For this reason God sends them a powerful delusion so that they will believe the lie . . .'.

How awesome and terrible that last statement is: but for the believer it should be encouragement to hold firmly to the truth of what is revealed to us in the Word of God.

A further major warning concerning counterfeit spiritual activity is found in Revelation 13:11–18, describing the second beast of John's vision. The first beast of that chapter corresponds to the man of sin, while the second is the 'false prophet', who is encountered again in Revelation 19:20. His function is to perform miraculous signs by power which counterfeits that of God, so as to deceive the people on earth into worshipping the man of sin. They will be fooled into thinking that he is the true Christ, but he will be the anti- or pseudo-Christ.

WARNINGS OF FALSE DOCTRINE

Jesus, Paul and John have all warned us concerning the dangers of counterfeit spiritual activity. There is also, however, a second major aspect of deception about which the Scriptures warn, and it is that of false doctrine. Paul speaks about it numerous times in his letters, for example in 2 Corinthians 11:1–4, in

Galatians 1:6–9 and in Colossians 2:8–23. He warns in 1 Timothy 4:1 that 'The Spirit clearly says that in later times some will abandon the faith and follow deceiving spirits and things taught by demons. Such teachings come through hypocritical liars . . .'. Let us be clear about what Paul is saying: it is a warning principally for the closing days of the age – 'later times'. It is a warning that Christians will fall away: you cannot abandon a faith unless you have first been a party to it. The false teachings will not be man-made, but demonically inspired by deceiving spirits, and they will come through people who are hypocrites and liars; like the 'savage wolves' of Acts 20:29–30, they will be falsely motivated so as to draw people away from the truth in order to obtain a following for themselves.

It is of vital importance in these days that we are alert to the dangers of false teaching. Those of us who teach must be diligent to declare the *whole* counsel of God; it was only on that basis that Paul was able to declare himself innocent of the blood of all who had heard him (Acts 20:26–27) and he was warning the elders of the church at Ephesus to be equally diligent. All believers should cultivate the habit of the 'noble Bereans' (Acts 17:11), who did not accept even the teaching of Paul as being true until they had examined it in the light of the Scriptures. How we in the church need in these days to re-examine our diet of the seemingly-endless flow of books and magazines, and to ensure that above all we are fully acquainted and familiar with the whole of the Bible. Only by knowing what is in God's Word can we walk in safety.

Paul's chief warning concerning false doctrine is found in 2 Timothy 4:1–4. He has just encouraged Timothy at the end of chapter 3 concerning the importance of holding fast to Scripture, underlining that '*all* Scripture is God-breathed . . . so that the man of God may be thoroughly equipped for every good work' (vv 16–17). We need to note that there are those in leadership in the church of God in these days who do not believe in the inspiration of Scripture; if they thus declare the Word of God to be untrue concerning itself, we must then question the validity of whatever else such men may say.

In chapter 4, Paul urges Timothy to preach the Word . . . 'with great patience and careful instruction' (v 2), particularly in the light of the fact that 'the time will come when men will not put up with sound doctrine. Instead, to suit their own desires, they will gather around them a great number of teachers to say what their itching ears want to hear. They will turn their ears away from the truth and turn aside to myths' (vv 3–4).

I believe we are now living in such days. A factor which has lately become of particular concern is the coming together of the two major facets of deception – counterfeit spiritual activity and false doctrine – in such a way as to support and reinforce one another. This brings great danger to the Body of Christ, particularly as many believers now have only a very limited knowledge of what is contained in the Bible. In Deuteronomy 13:1–5, the warning of Moses to the people of Israel is that they may encounter a prophet who predicts signs and wonders which do in fact come to pass – but that this in itself is not sufficient to validate him as a true man of God; for if he then teaches them falsely so as to lead them astray, he is to be regarded as a false prophet.

Biblically, therefore, the acid test of the genuineness of a man's ministry lies not in signs and wonders, nor even in accurate predictions, but in his faithfulness to the Lord in declaring doctrine which is in accordance with God's Word.

THE KANSAS CITY PROPHETS

In recent years, this biblical principle of giving preeminence to the revealed Word of God has been turned upside down. In 1990 came the experience of the Kansas City prophets. These men were brought to the charismatic church in Britain that year on a wave of publicity concerning their outstanding prophetic ministry, and particularly of a specific predictive prophecy that a great revival would break out in this country in October 1990. It did not, to the dismay and embarrassment of many church leaders who had publicly endorsed this ministry, and to the great disappointment of thousands of believers who had believed that their longings for revival were about to be realised and that they would see dramatic events.

This sort of happening is dishonouring to the name of the Lord, bringing his church into ridicule in the eyes of those who had been exposed to the extensive publicity, particularly in the mass media. It also undermines the belief that the Holy Spirit does bring genuine prophecy to the church for our upbuilding and enlightenment. Furthermore, the shock and disappointment has damaging and far-reaching effects. For many years God's people in the charismatic churches have been given by their leader's specific words of prophecy and much teaching of a prophetic nature which has been triumphalist in flavour, encouraging expectations of mighty visitations of God, of great numerical increase, and of the church enjoying an experience of exercising power and authority in the world, equipped with unparalleled supernatural spiritual power.

This kind of teaching has been entirely at odds with the biblical picture of a suffering servant church displaying the humility of her Master, preaching the gospel in the last days under increasing pressure and persecution. It brings with it a particular danger from which we are now, I believe, beginning to reap harmful results. Where leaders have continued to promise great things to the people and those promises have gone unfulfilled, the leaders come under an increasing sense of pressure to deliver the goods which have been promised; and the people's experience of disappointment, of hope continually deferred, leads to disillusionment. The scene is thus set for the entry of deception, because both leaders and people become desperate at the failed predictions and dashed hopes, and both are increasingly likely to grasp at any straw which appears at last to bring fulfilment. In such circumstances the counterfeit can all too easily succeed, because the need for something, anything, to fill the gap overrides the godly caution which should test and discern the source of what is being offered before it is accepted as genuine.

The doctrine brought by the Kansas City prophets was very much in line with the triumphalism of Restoration teaching and expectations. The teaching was based upon specific prophecies which have been reproduced in Chapter Five. It was that God was raising up in the church an 'end-time breed of dread warriors', before whose power and authority nothing would be able to stand. They would be an all-conquering army; and the scriptural basis for that teaching was taken from Joel 2:2–11. To base such a doctrine on that passage of Scripture, however, is entirely fallacious. Arising immediately from the preceding description of the effects of a great plague of locusts, the passage describes an all-consuming army invading the land of Israel, and taken in its context of 'the day of the Lord' (vv 1–2, 11) it is speaking prophetically of an invading army sent by God to execute his final judgment against Judah and Jerusalem at the end of the age. Certainly its fulfilment is yet in the future, at the time of Jacob's tribulation (Jer 30); but it does not refer to the church. Nowhere in Scripture does God call his church to be an invading army to execute judgment. Nor does it speak of a worldwide domination; the specific geographical setting is the land of Israel and in particular the city of Zion.

Such teaching, based on a complete distortion of this passage from the Word of God, displays the worst sort of error in interpretation. It takes specific predictive prophecy, converts it into an allegory which is not to be found in the text – that the invaders represent Christian 'dread warriors' – and then bases a doctrine upon that allegorical fancy. It is not merely nonsense, however. It is also dangerous to the church because of the numbers of leaders who received it with gladness and were willing to let their people believe such teaching.

Why should such false doctrine be so gladly and easily received? It was received gladly because it reinforced all the false doctrine and false prophecy which had been accepted during the previous fifteen years. It was also received easily, I believe, for a more subtle and deadly reason, which is to be found in the coming together to reinforce one another of the two main strands of deception, counterfeit spiritual manifestations and false teaching, to which I have already referred. Let us now consider the topic a little further.

The Kansas City prophets came to Britain as guests whose ministry was being invited and welcomed by many prominent church leaders in the country. Some of us had been unhappy about this visit, because we were not at ease with their style of ministry or their doctrine, and in particular we had said publicly that we did not believe the specific prophecy concerning the outbreak of revival in October 1990 to have come from the Lord.

During the summer of 1990 there was a preliminary gathering where the ministry of these men was presented to an invited group of national charismatic church leaders. Some remained unhappy and unconvinced, but others were willing at the end to sign a statement approving of the ministry as being valid. In view of the doctrine already mentioned, one might have expected the ministry to be regarded as questionable on those grounds with no further evidence being necessary; but there was a further ingredient involved.

An outstanding and spectacular feature of the ministry lay in the singling out by name from the public platform of individual members of the audience with whom the speaker was apparently not acquainted. Words of knowledge were given concerning those individuals, relating to aspects of their past life and their present circumstances, and usually completed with encouraging prophecy concerning their future. The accuracy of the words of knowledge brought amazement and served to convince many that they should attest the ministry as being from God.

To be convinced on these grounds alone, however, is to make an assumption which can be dangerously misleading. There is, of course, no question but that such words of knowledge could certainly have been given by revelation from the Holy Spirit; but we need to be alert to the fact that this is not the only possibility where supernatural spiritual activity is being manifested. It is essential also to take other factors into account in order to be sure of the source from which the manifestation originates. One factor, the nature of the doctrine, we have already mentioned; in addition there is the scriptural injunction to 'test the spirits' (1 John 4:1), and a further matter of vital importance is whether what is happening is consistent with the revelation of Scripture – is it in character for the God of the Bible to be acting in this sort of way? An understanding of the ways of God as revealed in his Word is of great importance: according to Psalm 95:10, quoted again in Hebrews 3:10, the hearts of God's people go astray when they do not know his ways.

We charismatic Christians can be terrifyingly gullible when it comes to supernatural spiritual manifestation. We assume that because a thing looks right, it is right. A good counterfeit always looks right unless and until it is put to the test. When a word of knowledge is true, we assume that this means that it must have come from God. That is an assumption which is unsafe to make, and one which the Word of God demonstrates to be so. In Acts 16:16–18, we find the following account of the experience of Paul and Silas with a slave girl who had a spirit of divination:

> Once when we were going to the place of prayer, we were met by a slave girl who had a spirit by which she predicted the future. She earned a great deal of money for her owners by fortune-telling. This girl followed Paul and the rest of us, shouting, 'These men are servants of the Most High God, who are telling you the way to be saved.' She kept this up for many days. Finally Paul became so troubled that he turned round and said to the spirit, 'In the name of Jesus Christ I command you to come out of her!' At that moment the spirit left her.

There was not one false word in the slave-girl's statement about Paul and Silas. The spirit of divination was speaking absolute factual truth through her. Yet Paul discerned that the source of her knowledge was false and commanded the evil spirit to leave her.

What a lesson this contains for us in these days. How much we need to be alert and discerning, aware of the subtleties of the Adversary. Satan has no objection to presenting us with any amount of factual truth, but always with a false motive. If true statements will cause us to lower our guard and be lulled into a false sense of security, then he will willingly use them to pave the way so that when the lie finally comes we will not detect it. If, by a spirit of divination, he can give us a number of accurate words of knowledge so as to convince us that God is the source from which this spiritual manifestation is coming, then he will gladly oblige; once we have made the mistaken assumption that all is from God and all is well, we will then without hesitation accept the false teaching which follows.

It is imperative that we learn the *ways* of God from Scripture. The doctrine of Joel's Army was false and the ministry should have been questioned on those grounds alone. In addition, however, we need to ask the question: 'Would Jesus in person be doing such a thing in such a way?' – specifically in this case, 'Would Jesus personally stand on a public platform and dispense words of knowledge for no apparent reason other than to display the fact that he had the ability to do so?' The answer in light of Scripture would be a resounding NO! Jesus was never willing to perform spiritual signs to order, as a performance for its own sake. He did so when it was necessary for the purpose of exercising the compassion of God towards the needy; the signs confirmed the truth of the Word which he spoke and they were certainly indications of his Messiahship, but he chose to communicate his authority through the words which he spoke, not through the signs and wonders. Indeed, Jesus often told those whom he healed to keep quiet about it. In these days, however, we are more impressed by the signs than by the truth of the Word and it brings us into great danger of deception. Believing without question or testing that the source of origin of the signs is genuine, we easily swallow the bait which has masked the hidden hook of false doctrine to bring us into error.

During the summer of 1990, the members of the ministry team of which I was part met together for a day to pray and wait upon the Lord about this perplexing matter of the then-impending visit of the Kansas City prophets. During that time, I received and shared a vivid mental picture. I saw first a large flat empty expanse of sand on a seashore. The sea was a very long way back down the beach, and scattered about on the sand were a number of large rocks, all of which seemed to be about four to five feet high. Each rock had a flat top on which was a small lighthouse.

The picture then changed. The rocks no longer supported lighthouses but were otherwise unaltered. The sands were covered with many people, enjoying themselves on the beach on a fine warm day. Then, as I watched, there came sweeping in across the sand a sudden very swift flood-tide. Nobody had time to get out of its way, except for some who scrambled onto the tall rocks and stood there, above the level of the water which seemed to be about three to four feet deep.

There was no panic from those in the water. After momentary surprise, they were splashing around and shouting to those who were up on the rocks: 'Come on in, the water's warm and it feels lovely', but those on the rocks were refusing, saying 'we don't trust it'.

Then, as suddenly as the flood-tide had come in, it receded back across the sands and all those in the water were swept out with it. The sands were now empty again except for those standing on the rocks, whom I saw had now become the lighthouses which I had first seen.

Asking the Lord what this meant, I received the understanding that the flood-tide signified a coming wave of deception; it was not the first and it would recede, but it would not be the last and further more potent waves of deception would come. Those who remained happily in the water were deceived by the fleshly appeal of what was happening to them, and their failure to discern the true nature of it and withdraw would mean that they would be easily swept into the next wave when it came, and further deceived. Those who stood on the rocks were those who stood on the rock of God's Word and distrusted what was suddenly happening, and they would continue to be as lighthouses of warning when further flood-tides came in to try to deceive God's people.

THE TORONTO EXPERIENCE

The phenomenon of Kansas City did recede, although it left behind a lot of confusion and unresolved issues, and I thought little about that picture again for some years. Then, in the early months of 1994, we began to hear of the amazing things which were being reported from Toronto. As the reports continued to flow in, I was being urged by many people to visit and experience what was happening there. Having no great desire to go and with a busy schedule, I resisted the idea for several months, but finally I was convinced that the Lord was requiring me to make the trip and I went to Toronto for a week's visit.

I arrived in Toronto on Friday 14th October, 1994 and attended meetings on the concluding days of the large 'Catch the Fire' conference which had been taking place during that week. These meetings took place in a large auditorium of a local hotel, which was capable of containing, I would guess, some two to three thousand people.

During the times of worship, I felt as if I were in a rock concert. The level of noise was deafening to the point of being physically painful and oppressive, and brought an increasing sense of unreality. This, together with the insistent rhythmic beat of the drums and of the bass guitar tends to induce a state bordering on hypnosis in susceptible people and creates a spiritual atmosphere in which I would say without hesitation that the demonic can thrive.

During these times of worship, many people began to exhibit jerking bodily movements which were unnatural. Some of these people appeared to be in a state of trance. From a number of years' experience of deliverance ministry, I would identify a good deal of what I saw as proceeding from demonic spirits associated with occult practices, particularly voodoo. There were some women near to where I was standing whose bodily movements were unmistakably those of increasing sexual excitement, reaching a point at which they fell to the floor. All of this was perhaps hardly surprising in an atmosphere which was really not unlike that of a pop concert in which the fans get worked up to an increasing height of frenzy. What disturbed me most was not that Satan was active – of course he always is – but the failure of leadership to distinguish between the spirits which were operating.

The teaching which I encountered in Toronto was to the effect that because God is doing a work amongst his people, therefore everything which takes place is by definition an activity of the Holy Spirit and it is assumed that Satan is inactive. I have never encountered any form of teaching which is more dangerous or which could open the door so widely to deception and the undetected activity of a demonic spirit. To make such an assumption is a total abdication of one of the principal responsibilities of Christian leadership. The warnings in Scripture about deception are being completely ignored and such teaching flies in the face of scriptural commands that when any form of spiritual activity is seen to be taking place, it is to be weighed and tested and an assessment is to be made as to whether its origin is truly from God.

The teaching from Toronto, however, sets aside the spiritual gift of distinguishing between spirits (1 Cor 12:10) and ignores the clear teaching of other scriptures. In 1 Corinthians 14:29 we are told that where prophecy is being spoken in the assembly of the church, we are to '*weigh carefully* what is said'. The words in italics are a translation of a Greek word which comes from exactly the same root as the word used in 1 Corinthians 12:10 for the discerning of, or distinguishing between, spirits.

The instruction of 1 Thessalonians 5:21–22, again in the context of spiritual manifestations, is that we should 'test everything. Hold on to the good. Avoid every kind of evil'. Here the Greek word translated 'test' has the meaning of examining a thing, putting it to the test to determine whether or not it is genuine; and the identical word is found in 1 John 4:1: 'Dear friends, do not believe every spirit, but *test* the spirits to see whether they are from God, because many false prophets have gone out into the world' (italics mine). The Word of God warns us consistently never to accept spiritual manifestations as being from the Holy Spirit unless their source has been put to the test by the body of believers and discerned to be genuine.

It is the height of folly and irresponsibility to ignore such scriptures in days when not only the activity of God but also the activity of Satan is becoming greater and more widespread. If we are to accept that in some particular situation such as this, it is in order for discernment to be discarded, where will such a teaching end? How are we to know where, if at all, we should draw the line? The warnings of Scripture in, for example, 2 Thessalonians 2:9–10 and Revelation 13:13–14, are now coming all too close for comfort, and a church which had not learned to distinguish between good and evil (Heb 5:14) will be a target for any kind of deception which begins to take place. I am concerned about the demonic activity which I saw taking place in some people in Toronto, but I am far more alarmed at the potential results of this particular line of teaching.

LAYING ON OF HANDS

On a number of occasions since my visit to Toronto, believers have requested prayer at the conclusion of a meeting at which I have spoken. They have done so because they had previously submitted to laying on of hands in order to receive the 'Toronto Blessing', and had since felt unaccountably troubled in spirit in a way which had previously been foreign to them. Every such person to whom I have ministered has shown evidence of being under demonic oppression and has received specific deliverance in the Name of the Lord Jesus Christ.

This is not of course to suggest that all those who have had contact with the Toronto Blessing have come into spiritual bondage; to jump to such a conclusion would be entirely unwarranted. What has seemed to me to be of considerable significance, however, is the repeated combination of two factors. In every one of these cases, the person for whom I have been asked to pray had first received a spiritual impartation by means of the laying on of hands by another person who had themselves already received it; and secondly, had subsequently become disturbed in spirit in a way which they had not experienced before.

I believe these facts should draw our attention to an issue which is of greater importance than perhaps we have previously realised. A few days before I went to Toronto, I was waiting upon the Lord and was given a short word of encouragement and instruction. I wrote it down, and now quote a passage whose relevance has become increasingly apparent:

> Do not accept the laying on of hands from anyone except those whom you know from experience to be trustworthy and to have my Spirit within them. To submit voluntarily to the laying on of hands is to submit to the spiritual power that is within a man. When this power is that of the Holy Spirit, then you will receive blessing through that which is good; but where it is not, evil can be transferred.

More recently my attention has been drawn to the lesson contained in Haggai 2:10–14. In it, two questions are posed. The first is whether if consecrated meat comes in contact with other food, the consecration is thereby transferred to the unconsecrated food; and the answer is that it is not. The second question is whether if a person who is ceremonially defiled through contact with a dead body touches food, that defilement is transferred to the food so that it also becomes defiled; the answer this time is affirmative.

The message is plain: spiritual **consecration** cannot be transferred by physical contact, as in the laying on of hands. If a man has received spiritual blessing, he cannot pass it on to another in this way. (If he is spiritually undefiled and lays hands on another, the Holy Spirit may move directly upon that other person – but where that is the case, there is no spiritual transference taking place between the persons themselves.)

Spiritual **defilement** however, can be transferred from one to another through physical contact. It is well established, for example, that such a transference of spirits can take place through illicit sexual activity. If one man has come under the influence of an evil spirit, the influence can be transferred to another who submits voluntarily to the laying on of his hands. We need to beware of careless practices and to exercise godly vigilance and caution. Paul warns: 'Do not be hasty in the laying on of hands, and do not share in the sins of others. Keep yourself pure' (1 Tim 5:22). It is imperative for our safety that we take heed to the instructions of Scripture; they are given for the protection and well-being of the whole Body.

MISUSE OF THE WORD OF GOD

While I was at Toronto, and even more in the months which have followed, I have had an increasing concern – to the point of considerable alarm – at the ways in which the Word of God is now being mishandled by many leaders in the charismatic churches. The misuse and distortion of Scripture in order to try to justify bizarre spiritual manifestations with some sort of theological explanation has been appalling; it has been as if attempts were being made to underpin a collapsing building with any piece of rubble which comes to hand.

The difficulty has been that the 'building' in question does not have any foundation in Scripture, however desperate the attempts to find one. At the Airport Vineyard Fellowship in Toronto, I heard the Pastor give a message in which he declared that Isaiah 25:6 was a description of what God was currently doing – God was in 'feasting mode'. Yet that scripture has no possible relevance to any present situation; it is lifted straight out of the context of an apocalyptic passage relating to the events of the Day of the Lord and what will happen at the Second Coming of Christ.

Again, in the course of the same message, he made reference to the parable of the Prodigal Son in Luke 15:11–32, and declared that it teaches that God loves any opportunity to hold a party. Yet its emphasis is nothing of the sort, but rather the greatness of God's fatherly forgiveness and restoration of a repentant sinner.

A further example of such extraordinary misuse of Scripture came when a prominent Anglican leader visited a church where I have a friend in leadership. His message consisted of encouragement to welcome unusual spiritual manifestations, including the making of animal noises, and it was based on one sentence taken out of Isaiah 28:21: 'to do his work, his strange work'. These few words, again lifted out of context, were declared to justify the idea that the bizarre activities were a 'strange work' which God is doing in these days, and that they should therefore be accepted without further question. But in the context, what is actually being described is a work of judgment and destruction by God against his own covenant people of Israel, and it is to him a 'strange work', and an 'alien task', because it is foreign and abhorrent to God's normal desire to bless his people and to act in mercy rather than in judgment. Theologically, this sort of teaching has no validity.

DRUNK IN THE SPIRIT

The strange and unco-ordinated behaviour of many who have been touched by the Toronto experience has frequently been described as being due to people being 'drunk in the Spirit'. I have myself for many years been familiar with the phenomenon of people who are receiving ministry from the Holy Spirit experiencing loss of bodily strength so as to be temporarily too weak to rise from their chair or from the floor; indeed, I also have had the same experience. Never before, however, have I seen the spectacle of people staggering about, slurring their speech and showing other characteristic signs normally associated with alcoholic intoxication.

The concept that a person can be 'drunk in the Spirit' is one of which Scripture knows nothing. Two passages have been used frequently to try to justify the idea, but they entirely fail to do so when subjected to proper interpretation. In Acts 2:1–13, what is being described is the phenomenon, historically unprecedented and utterly amazing, of about 120 people suddenly beginning to declare the wonders of God in a host of different foreign languages. It was only those who mocked what was happening who suggested drunkenness as the cause, but the majority of the onlookers were simply described, understandably enough, as 'amazed and perplexed'. There is no suggestion whatever of any behaviour which justified the description of physical drunkenness, and to try to read it into the text is to abuse the Word of God. Is Peter's sermon that of a drunken man?

The second scripture used in this context is Ephesians 5:18, but it says nothing whatever about being drunk in the Spirit. Indeed, coming at the end of a lengthy passage urging the believer to avoid ungodly behaviour, it would be astonishing if it did! The verse forbids being drunk (literally 'soaked') with wine, the *evidence* of which is debauched (literally 'unsaved') behaviour (v18). Instead, believers are to be *filled* with the Spirit – the Greek verb used is *pleróo*, which had nothing to do with drunkenness – and the *evidence* of being in that condition is that they will produce psalms, hymns and spiritual songs (v 19), thanksgiving to God (v 20), and submission to one another out of reverence for Christ (v 21), not slurred speech and drunken behaviour!

Everywhere in Scripture, drunkenness is condemned as ungodly. How can we therefore accept that the Spirit of God would deliberately bring about in a believer the evidence of drunken behaviour as if he were intoxicated with alcohol? The thing is utterly unthinkable, unless one discards the consistent teaching of the Word of God as irrelevant. Sadly, and most frightening of all, this is what some charismatic leaders are now beginning to do.

EXTRA-BIBLICAL EXPERIENCE

Animal noises, convulsions, bodily jerkings, loss of speech-control, and the like, are being described as 'extra-biblical' phenomena – which they certainly are. This feature of the activities should, however, put an immediate question-mark over their authenticity; normally, unbiblical experience is found to emanate, not from the Holy Spirit, but from the realm of the demonic. But among many leaders no such questioning is taking place; but rather the reverse. It has even been suggested that the spiritual experiences and the manifestations of the Holy Spirit recorded in the pages of the New Testament were the experience of the church in its infancy in those early days; but that now in our day the church is being brought into maturity and we must therefore expect experiences from God which were unknown to the early church and therefore not to be found in the Bible. We are consequently in uncharted waters, being led solely by the Spirit. This opens the church to precisely the danger which Paul defines in Ephesians 4:14.

This sort of teaching, if pursued to its logical conclusion, is the height of dangerous folly. It is like saying that our maps are no longer of use to us because we have gone beyond their boundaries. We can no longer check our course, but must trust that any wind which happens to blow will take us in the right direction. We have discarded, however, all means of knowing either where the wind is coming from or the direction in which we are heading. In fact, we are drifting helplessly at the mercy of any force which may influence us.

A teaching which discards the Bible as the final authority for the validity of Christian experience is a teaching which emanates straight from the master of deception himself. It tears down the boundary walls which God has erected for the safety of his people, and it opens the door wide for the charismatic church to join in an unwitting embrace with the New Age movement and all its occult activities. I have already had reported to me instances of levitation occurring at 'Toronto'-type meetings at a church in the north of England. Where will the line be drawn? On the basis of this sort of thinking and teaching, why should not telepathy or astral travel or any other occult practices be embraced under the deception that they are God's latest blessings to his maturing church? Unless there is repentance and a return to an acknowledgment of the supreme and ultimate authority of the Word of God, the church is being led into a place of great spiritual peril.

THE NEED FOR REPENTANCE

Reflection upon the history of the charismatic renewal movement as I have experienced it, leads me to the conclusion that we began well, but that increasingly we have departed from the purposes of God. We have done this as a result of having moved progressively farther from an adherence to his Word, a process which has accelerated alarmingly during the last decade. I believe we are in imminent danger, if the trend is not checked, of reaching a point where we can no longer be said to care about biblical truth, but only about enticing experiences. Repentance is urgently needed in order that God should not finally give us up to the delusion which we seem to desire more than the truth of the Word.

The triumphalist teachings of Dominion theology lead inevitably to a post-millennialist view of eschatology; and with this comes also a rejection of the consistent testimony of Scripture concerning God's intention to fulfil all his stated purposes for the nation of Israel. To deny those purposes and to declare the church to have replaced the descendants of Jacob as the inheritor of all the covenant promises of God makes out his Word to be a lie and distorts its testimony.

This issue is of fundamental importance. Taking his farewell of the elders of the Ephesian church, Paul declared, 'I am innocent of the blood of all men. For I did not shrink from declaring to you the whole purpose of God' (Acts 20:26–27, NASB). We can only have a right understanding of the will and purpose of God for the church in the days in which we live if we accept as truth the whole of the revelation contained in Scripture, but a false hope of revival and rulership here and now has been substituted for the true biblical hope of the Second Coming of Jesus and the establishment of the Messianic Kingdom. Unbiblical doctrine gives rise to unbiblical expectations and opens the door to increasing error and deception.

SPIRITUAL DISCERNMENT

What could and should have saved us from getting to the position we have now reached? I have no doubt in my own mind that the phenomenon of the 'Toronto Blessing' constitutes the next experience of a flood-tide of deception such as I was shown at the time of the Kansas City prophets. What will come next? We are in increasing danger.

We would not have fallen prey to the confusion brought into the church by successive waves of deception if we had known and applied the principles of spiritual discernment given to us in the pages of Scripture. We have already referred to the test as to whether spiritual activity conforms to God's *ways* as revealed in the Bible.

When in Toronto, I heard given consistently from the public platform the injunction that people should not feel the need to weigh and test anything that was happening: that it was all from God, who was present in such a powerful way that Satan could not gain access. People should therefore 'open up their minds, put down their defences and go with the flow'.

Not only is this utter folly; it is also plain disobedience to the Lord – clearly contradicting the command contained in his Word. Satan is the 'prince of the power of the air' (Eph 2:2 RSV) and we can never safely assume on this earth that he is denied access. Therefore, the church is instructed in all gatherings, particularly where spiritual manifestations are taking place, to be alert and on guard: 'Do not put out the Spirit's fire; do not treat prophecies with contempt. *Test everything. Hold on to the good. Avoid every kind of evil'* (1 Thess 5:19–22).

What exactly are we testing? Our principal concern is to test *the source of origin* from which the spiritual activity is proceeding, be it prophecy, tongues, healing, or whatever. Our principal question is: what manner of spirit is operating behind and inspiring this activity? Is it the Holy Spirit? If so, all is well; but if not, we must be on guard and refuse to accept the activity as valid.

An obvious and immediate test is that of the Word of God. Does the utterance, or teaching, or activity conform to the revelation of Scripture? If not, we may dismiss it at once.

We are also commanded to test the spirits and not to be so gullible as to believe that every spirit is from God (1 John 4:1). How may we do this?

Acknowledgment of Jesus

1 John 4:2–3 – If a spirit does not acknowledge that Jesus Christ has come in the flesh it is not from God, but is the spirit of the antichrist.

Learn to recognise

1 John 2:20–21, 26–27 – But you have an anointing from the Holy One, and all of you know the truth. I do not write to you because you do not know the truth, but because you do know it and because no lie comes from the truth . . . I am writing these things to you about those who are trying to lead you astray. As for you, the anointing you received from him remains in you, and you do not need anyone to teach you. But as his anointing teaches you about all things and as that anointing is real, not counterfeit – just as it has taught you, remain in him.

Every believer who has received the Holy Spirit has this anointing from the Lord. It has the effect upon us that our own spirits have the capacity to recognise what is true, genuinely from the Lord, and what is not. As Jesus said (John 10:3–5), his sheep *know* his voice and can distinguish it from a stranger's voice.

Unfortunately, very few believers have been taught to recognise and to respond to the witness of their own spirits within them. Most of us will probably have experienced the sense of the inward lifting or rising of our spirit when something is genuinely from the Lord; and conversely the sense of deadness or heaviness, or even alarm-bells, when the source is not from God. However, many believers tend to ignore or quench that inner witness, often because they rely on leadership to do all the discerning; or because they think that a trusted minister cannot get it wrong, so their own discernment must be at fault. Anybody can be in error, and we should never take anything for granted. It is for *all* Christians to take heed of the inner witness with which the Lord has supplied us; and if we do so, it leads to the safety of the whole Body. This inner witness is often the first indication we receive in any particular situation of whether the Holy Spirit is active, or perhaps simply a human spirit operating in the flesh, or sometimes a demonic spirit. It is of great importance.

Distinguish between spirits

1 Corinthians 12:10 – The Holy Spirit manifests through believers 'the ability to distinguish between spirits'. This is the witness given directly from the Holy Spirit through one or more believers to enable us to identify the spirits operating in a situation – to receive the awareness of what manner of spirit is active. If it is not from God, then it may be, for example, a lying spirit, an unclean spirit, a seducing spirit, a spirit of pride, or greed, or whatever else may be at work. Through this gift the Holy Spirit reveals

to God's people the exact type of demonic activity which is opposing them.

The operation of this gift is of vital importance in any situation of supernatural spiritual activity. Any believer may be used by the Holy Spirit in this way and it is a great mistake to rely solely on the leaders, or for leaders to seek to keep all matters of discernment within their own hands.

Put to the test

1 Corinthians 14:29 – Where prophecy in particular is concerned there must be a careful weighing of what is said. Of all spiritual manifestations, prophecy is potentially both the most valuable and also the most dangerous, because of its great capacity either to edify or to mislead those who hear and receive it as being a direct communication of the mind of God. The same root word is used as in 1 Corinthians 12:10 – the Greek verb *diakrino*, meaning 'to distinguish, to make a separation' between true and false. When prophecy is weighed, both the content of what is spoken and the spirit responsible for inspiring the utterance should be put to the test of both the witness of the Holy Spirit and the inner witness of the spirits of those who are present.

Practise discernment

Finally, we should take notice of Hebrews 5:14 – '. . . solid food is for the mature, who by constant use have trained themselves to distinguish good from evil'.

Again the verb *diakrino* is used. God wants all believers to come to maturity, and continual alertness to distinguish what is of God from what is not is a hallmark of a mature believer. Practising discernment in the ways which the Bible reveals should be a way of life for a Christian.

If these ways of discernment had been taught and practised within the charismatic churches in the way which the Bible instructs and encourages, much deception and difficulty could have been avoided. The hour is late and deception has made deep inroads, but my plea is that we might embrace repentance in these areas while there is yet time. If we return wholeheartedly to the Word of God as final and unquestioned authority in all matters; if we embrace the biblical teaching concerning the nation of Israel; and if we become diligent to distinguish the genuine activity of the Holy Spirit from all other manifestations, then surely the Lord will deliver us from error, and instead of the Ishmael which we have produced, will bring forth for us the Isaac of his original purpose.

CHAPTER SEVEN

HERE TODAY, WHERE TOMORROW?

The twentieth century will surely go down in history as the century of the Holy Spirit, both due to the amazing worldwide expansion of the Pentecostal movement from the beginning of the century and the charismatic renewal which has swept across the world in the second half of the century. But will it be seen as the pure work of God representing a turning point in world history? Or will it be seen as a missed opportunity, a work of God spoiled by human hands?

It was often a cry of the prophets of Israel that the nation had moved outside the blessing. The people had deviated from the path set before them by God. They had neglected his Word, spurned his law and disobeyed his commands. Therefore the nation was experiencing judgment rather than blessing. They had brought upon themselves the antithesis of blessing clearly foreseen by Moses in the warnings given, 'If you do not obey the LORD your God and do not carefully follow all his commands and decrees I am giving you today, all these curses will come upon you and overtake you: You will be cursed in the city and cursed in the country . . .' (Deut 28:15–16).

The biblical record of God's relationship with Israel

shows that it was always God's delight to bless his people. This is his intention today just as it was when he called Israel to be his people through whom he could reveal himself to the world and establish them as his servant. 'I will also make you a light for the Gentiles, that you may bring my salvation to the ends of the earth' (Is 49:6).

The 'Great Commission' given by Jesus to his disciples to preach the gospel to all nations reaffirmed God's intention (Matt 28:19). His promise to send the Holy Spirit was to enable the church to carry out his command: 'You will receive power when the Holy Spirit comes on you; and you will be my witnesses in Jerusalem, and in all Judea and Samaria, and to the ends of the earth' (Acts 1:8).

The fresh outpouring of the Holy Spirit upon the church at the beginning of the twentieth century, which resulted in the worldwide Pentecostal movement, is a significant milestone enabling us to understand how God is working out his purposes in our times. As the church has progressed, two things have happened of immense significance. The first is that the worldwide church has grown at a phenomenal rate. The majority of this growth has been in the poorer non-industrial nations. David Barrett in the *Encyclopaedia of World Religions* records that in 1900 only 17% of Christians were in the non-western nations.[1] By 1988 this had risen to 53% and he estimates that by the year 2000 this will have risen to 61% with only 32% in the rich western nations. The second significant fact is that the Holy Spirit has been renewing and revitalising the life of the traditional churches in the western world. This did not begin to happen until the second half of the twentieth century.[2]

It surely cannot be a mere coincidence that throughout this century a combination of disturbing and destructive social, economic and political forces have been moving with increasing velocity across the world. It has been a century of revolution, of war, terrorism and violence, as well as a century of incredible social and technological change which has been responsible for almost unbelievable upheavals in every continent and in almost every nation – China, Russia, the Indian sub-continent, the Middle East, every part of Africa, eastern Europe. The political upheavals which have shaken these nations have been matched by the revolutionary social forces that have swept away the foundations of social stability in most of the western nations.[3]

There are strong links between these events and the kind of eschatological scenario described in Scripture. Jesus gave a number of specific signs which would mark the nearness of his own Second Coming. They are to be found in Matthew 24 and Luke 21. There are additionally many passages both in the New Testament and in the Old Testament prophets that set the scene for the prelude of the 'Day of the Lord' when he will come to judge the nations.

It is not our purpose to elaborate that theme here, but it is relevant to note that world events towards the end of the second millennium are becoming increasingly like the biblical eschatological scenario. Paul tells us in Ephesians 3:10 that it is God's intention to use the church to reveal himself to the whole universe. It is his purpose to prepare a holy people, a people who love him and trust him and who are empowered by the Holy Spirit to declare his Word to the nations.

The Holy Spirit is given to the church for just this purpose, to enable the church to be the prophet to the world, to prepare the way of the Lord and to preach the gospel of salvation with power and authority, with signs and wonders following. But God can only use a purified people. When his people depart from his ways and run after the values of the world he withdraws his blessing and eventually removes his presence, leaving them unprotected from the onslaught of the enemy. There are many indications that this is what we are seeing in the western nations and also in western churches. We urgently need to learn the lessons recorded in the Old Testament.

BLESSING AND JUDGMENT

The history of Israel follows a constant cycle of blessing and judgment corresponding to the spiritual health of the nation as measured by the plumb-line of the people's faithfulness to the Word of God. Whenever God blessed the nation and a time of peace and prosperity was being enjoyed, it was not long before the people became unfaithful and turned away from God. Then things began to go wrong because the Lord gradually withdrew his blessing and the cover of his protection. Hosea has a telling passage which describes this process. He records what is essentially a lament of the Lord,

> 'I am the LORD your God,
> who brought you out of Egypt,
> You shall acknowledge no God but me,
> no Saviour except me.
> I cared for you in the desert,
> in the land of burning heat.
> When I fed them, they were satisfied;
> when they were satisfied, they became proud;
> then they forgot me.'
>
> (Hos 13:4–5)

Hosea was writing shortly before the fall of Samaria and the destruction of the northern kingdom of Israel and their exile in Assyria. He rightly interpreted the warning signs as things began to go wrong. He knew that the final tragedy would follow the withdrawal of the protecting hand of God when he finally turned his back upon his people leaving them exposed to their enemies. Ezekiel saw this in a vision of the Spirit of God leaving the temple in Jerusalem. He saw the word *Ichabod* 'Glory departed' over the city.

Thus blessing and judgment were always part of Israel's experience and are written across every page of her history. They illustrate important spiritual principles which are valid for all time for those who would be the people of God and who desire to experience his blessing. When we turn away from the Word of God, embracing false teaching and false prophecy, the consequences for the whole nation are serious and may even be disastrous as in the history of Israel. False teaching and prophecy pollute the spiritual life of the church, distort our discernment and fail to give moral and spiritual correction to the nation. The political, economic and social life of the nation becomes corrupted and standards fall. The ways of God revealed in the Bible also teach us that God holds his servants, particularly the religious leaders, responsible for the state of the nation.

THE BRITISH SITUATION

In Britain we are still suffering from the consequences of false prophecy given very publicly by the Kansas City prophets in 1990. Reference has already been made to this in earlier chapters but it is of sufficient importance to warrant further consideration since this marks a major turning point in the history and direction of the charismatic movement in Britain.

Bob Jones, Paul Cain and John Paul Jackson all

proclaimed that a mighty revival would be experienced in Britain in 1990, saying that it would spread across England into Scotland and then across the North Sea and throughout Europe. Paul Cain was even more explicit, stating that the revival would begin in London in October 1990 when John Wimber was due to lead a mission at the Docklands Conference Centre, East London.[4]

Just as Hananiah's false prophecy (Jer 28) came as a welcome relief from the stern message which Jeremiah had been preaching for a number of years, so this promise of revival came as sweet, enchanting music to the ears of many faithful believers who were longing for revival and had been interceding earnestly for many years. But they were misled. It was a false prophecy. I said so publicly six months before the October conference.[5] I had personal contact with all three men, including face-to-face discussions. But the band wagon was already rolling with, what was by British standards, extraordinary hype.

Tens of thousands flocked to hear these men with a popular message as they travelled across the country touring the provinces before their big London event. By the time of the Docklands Conference expectations were running high and before the end of the week they reached fever pitch with John Wimber commanding the Holy Spirit to come down. But God did not come upon his people in power like a mighty rushing wind as at Pentecost. The Holy Spirit does not obey the commands of men!

There were many signs that Britain was not yet ready for revival. For a number of years it had been apparent that God was shaking the nations in order to shake the confidence of mankind in material things and cause the nations to turn to him, the living God, to heed his Word and to walk in the paths of righteousness. Then in due time the blessing of God would be poured out upon nations that turned to him. The scripture underlying this hope was, '"In a little while I will once more shake the heavens and the earth, the sea and the dry land. I will shake all nations, and the desired of all nations will come, and I will fill this house with glory," says the LORD Almighty' (Hag 2:6–7).

1990 was too soon for a great revival. The boom years of the 1980s had to be followed by the bust years of the 1990s. The pride and complacency engendered by the success of the greedy acquisitive policies of the 1980s had to be broken. The corruption that accompanied the greed in the commercial and financial institutions had to be exposed. It can now be plainly seen that the seed sown in the 1980s has reaped a bitter harvest in the 1990s. But this was all part of God's intention to allow evil to reap its own reward and to bring about a humbling of powerful leaders in the political and business life of the nation.

The exposure of greed and corruption in the 1990s has brought about some dramatic revelations much capitalised on by the media, always hungry for sensation. The revelations have included adultery and bizarre sexual activities by politicians, the shaking of Lloyd's insurance underwriters and the plight of their 'names', the failure of a number of banking institutions and financial enterprises with attendant scandals such as BCCI, Barlow Clowes, the Guinness affair, the Maxwell affair and the collapse of Barings, one of the oldest and most respected family banks in England. The shaking of the financial heart of the economy also revealed vast salaries paid to individual managers in industry while at the same time large numbers of householders were unable to pay their mortgages and were losing their homes, and many businesses were going bankrupt.

This is all part of the shaking of the nation which

prepares the way for the gospel, in just the same way as a farmer prepares the ground to receive the seed so that it may take root and bear fruit, giving an abundant harvest. Prophecy plays an important part in the preparation for the Word of God by giving the spiritual interpretation of physical events. There are numerous examples of this in Scripture, such as Jeremiah's explanation for the withholding of the spring rains (Jer 3:3), and the powerful explanation given by Amos of drought, blight, plagues and other disasters (Amos 4:6–12).

It has always been God's intention that his church should be the prophet to the nation declaring his unchangeable Word in a changing world and making it applicable to each generation so that the will and purposes of God can be readily understood. It is the responsibility of those who exercise a prophetic ministry to be the eyes and ears of the church, to interpret events in accordance with principles laid down in Scripture so that the whole church can carry out its prophetic function in the nation, turning the people back to God when they have gone astray and leading the nation into the paths of righteousness where the blessing of God will be experienced. It is for this reason that the Holy Spirit has been poured out afresh in the twentieth century and that New Testament ministries have been restored.

THE KANSAS CITY PROPHETS

When the Kansas City prophets came, with their popular message of imminent revival, they also brought a teaching about prophecy which was contrary to Scripture and highly dangerous. This teaching focused upon signs and wonders thus hyping the supernatural and sensationalising the prophetic ministry in a way that is totally foreign to the Bible.

In May 1990, David Pytches published the book, *Some Said it Thundered*, which was timed to prepare the way for the visit of the Kansas City prophets. The book catalogued their paranormal experiences, all of which were uncritically accepted as being the work of the Holy Spirit. In fact, in his opening chapter, David Pytches referred to his first meeting with these men saying, 'It blew my mind'.

This is a very serious admission for a church leader to make. There was a great need for clear thinking and the application of biblical principles to test this new spiritual phenomenon. David Pytches clearly failed to do this and therefore opened the way for deception to enter the church. His book made no attempt to evaluate the supernatural occurrences reported. They were simply presented as the latest in signs and wonders to sweep across the charismatic horizon.

Typical of the incidents reported was the following account of a telephone conversation between Paul Cain and Mike Bickle. After the opening greetings Paul Cain said, 'Why, Mike, you've got a bit of a sniffle and you are all wet. Your hair is standing up on the left side of your head'. Bickle called his wife, Diana, to look at him. 'Sweetheart, Paul says I have a "sniffle", I am all wet and my hair is standing up on one side, Am I all wet?' 'Yes', she said. 'You have just come out of the shower!' 'And is my hair standing up on one side?' 'Yes', she replied, 'on the left side!' Paul Cain calls these strange experiences, 'little tokens that the line is still open with the Lord'.[6]

Pytches simply accepted this as divine revelation without asking the question, 'Why would the God of all creation, the Father of our Lord Jesus, reveal to a prophet that his pastor had just taken a shower?' This was not merely a trivialisation of prophecy, there was no consideration of the fact that this could have been 'divination' and that this is the way false prophets operate, to confound the unwary and exercise a controlling spirit over them.

Cain was hailed in *Some Said it Thundered* as a 'present-day prophet' who received 'a high level of revelation from God'.[7] In the book, David Pytches admitted that Cain was a disciple of William Branham and that 'there was always a special bond' between the two men but he failed to mention that Branham was rejected by the Assemblies of God for heresy. His preaching was similar to the Arian heresy that troubled the early church. Like Arius, Branham denied the Trinity, the divinity of Christ, the person of the Holy Spirit and other fundamental tenets of the Christian faith. He claimed that his remarkable healing ministry was channelled through 'an angel' rather than the Holy Spirit.

Paul Cain still describes Branham as 'the greatest prophet of the twentieth century' despite his record of heresy and neo-occultism. Cain himself claims that he is given supernatural knowledge through an angel and it would appear from his own testimony that his bond with Branham was never broken. Even more significantly, in 1989 Wimber announced that he himself was 'bonded to Paul Cain for life'. He did in fact break that bond a few years later, when his own health broke down and Cain fell from favour in the US following his prediction that the election of President Clinton would usher in an era of great blessing and a return to biblical morality in the USA and that Clinton himself would be the greatest president since Abraham Lincoln. Cain's popularity-rating further dropped after a visit to Iraq in the wake of the Gulf War when he was reported as saying that Saddam

Hussein was a good man greatly misunderstood and unjustly treated by the western nations.

Bob Jones, the senior Kansas City Fellowship prophet, was reported in *Some Said it Thundered* to receive thousands of angelic visitations, appearances of Jesus and out-of-body experiences, and audibly to hear the voice of God. Jones was presented to the British public, both in the book and in his appearances at Holy Trinity, Brompton in July 1990, as a prophet of extraordinary insight, despite the fact that those who knew his record were aware that his paranormal spiritual experiences began in a mental asylum where he had been committed following a lifestyle of alcoholism, violence, fornication and drug abuse. It was while there that, according to his own testimony, he was visited by demons who in 1990 were still appearing to him and with whom he claimed to hold conversations.[8]

I visited Jones in his home in Kansas City in 1989 and was immediately aware of a demonic presence. I subsequently told him directly that I did not believe him to be a prophet and that he should cease deceiving the church. It was very clear to me that Bob Jones was working through an evil spirit which he attempted to pass on to me through a form of 'laying on of hands' which I had not previously encountered. I was taken to see Jones by Jim Goll, one of the Kansas City Fellowship's pastoral staff, also said to be a prophet. At that time I had no knowledge of Jones' background, but it was this experience in Jones' home that raised doubts in my mind regarding Paul Cain's prophetic gifting. If Paul Cain really had the spiritual gifting he claimed, why was he not alerted to the presence of an evil spirit in Bob Jones' life?

I was dismayed when I heard that Jones was to be included in the team John Wimber brought to England in July 1990. At that point I was faced with a dilemma. How could I alert the church to my experience in Kansas City? I had already informed those responsible for the visit to Britain, but my warnings had been brushed aside. Many years' experience in the pastoral ministry has taught me the importance of personal relationships and I especially covet right relationships with other ministers. I believe strongly in following the principles of Matthew 18 (namely; going first to the brother with whom there is a problem, if it cannot be solved privately then drawing in one or two others and finally as a last resort going to the church).[9]

In December 1989 and January 1990 I had several meetings and telephone conversations with David Pytches, reporting what I and two colleagues (one, a man with an established international ministry) had experienced during our visit to Kansas City. David Pytches had invited me to write the Foreword to *Some Said it Thundered* but when he heard our report and my strong advice against publication, he withdrew the invitation and I was not able to see the book until after it was published in May 1990.

I subsequently learned that John Wimber had also advised against writing the book, saying that it was too soon to expose a new ministry to the public. When Pytches went ahead and wrote it, Wimber again appealed to him not to publish it, but he was determined to have it available before the visit of the Kansas City prophets who he and Sandy Millar were sponsoring at Holy Trinity, Brompton in July 1990. After *Some Said it Thundered* was published, Mike Bickle sent Pytches a sixty-minute tape outlining the numerous inaccuracies he had noted. At the same time I published an extensive critique in *Prophecy Today* questioning the accuracy of many of the incidents which were sensationalised in the book and using the teaching of the New Testament to question their validity.[10]

I followed the Matthew 18 principles carefully and throughout 1990 had extensive correspondence, telephone calls and face-to-face meetings with John Wimber, Mike Bickle, Paul Cain, Bob Jones, John Paul Jackson, as well as with David Pytches, Sandy Millar and many other British church leaders. It would not be ethical to reveal the detail of any of these private meetings and I only refer to them to demonstrate my commitment to maintaining unity in the church and brotherly relationships within the Body of Christ.

There comes a point where, when all private means have been exhausted, false teaching and practice have to be exposed in order to 'contend for the faith' and to protect the church from heresy. The New Testament shows the apostles constantly struggling to maintain the truth of the gospel. Paul warned the Corinthians about the danger of receiving anyone who 'comes to you and preaches a Jesus other than the Jesus we preached, or if you receive a different spirit from the one you received, or a different gospel from the one you accepted' (2 Cor 11:4). John, writing to the Seven Churches in Asia conveying the message of Jesus, did not hesitate to name those who were troubling the church with false teaching; the Nicolaitans in Ephesus and Pergamon and 'that woman Jezebel' in Thyatira (Rev 2:20).

Jones was presented to the churches in Britain by David Pytches and Sandy Millar, sponsors of the 1990 tour, as a genuine prophet of the Lord. He was sensationally written up as having accurate powers of prediction in *Some Said it Thundered* despite the fact that I had given David Pytches, both verbally and in writing, clear warnings about him before the manuscript was accepted for publication.

In two issues of *Prophecy Today* I referred to Bob Jones' occult connections. These were never refuted by the Vineyard/Kansas City Fellowship leadership. A report issued by Ernest Gruen (minister of one of the largest evangelical/charismatic churches in Kansas City) with the support of more than forty local ministers charged Jones with prophesying through a familiar spirit.

Wimber was aware of the demonic influence in Jones' life and because of this he did not allow him to minister publicly with him on the platform in London. He only allowed Jones to minister privately to leaders. It was highly unfortunate that the preachers to whom Jones prophesied were not told of his occult connection. They were therefore not alerted to the possibility that they might be receiving a message which was not from God, and were thus exposed to deception. The following year, 1991, Jones was dismissed from ministry after being exposed for what Wimber described as 'gross sexual sin' and a variety of other offences. He had been misusing his so-called 'prophetic powers' to solicit sexual favours from women.

The allegations listed by Wimber against Jones also included 'using the gifts to manipulate people for his personal desires, rebelling against pastoral authority, slandering leaders and the promotion of bitterness in the Body of Christ'. This was just part of a lengthy list of Jones' moral failures which Wimber and Bickle sent to a number of church leaders and Christian media around the world. Such a catalogue of moral and spiritual failures could surely not have been perpetrated in the one year since his ministering in Britain.

Wimber took an enormous risk in bringing Jones to Britain in July 1990, since he was aware of his occult problem. There has to be a powerful reason why he was included in the team. Jones was needed because it was his 'prophetic' powers that validated the whole Kansas City Fellowship ministry which had now been embraced by Vineyard. It was he who had prophesied over the fellowship in their earliest days. As a sign that they would have a worldwide prophetic ministry he declared that there would be a three-month drought in Kansas City. That prophecy was given on 28 May 1983 and Jones further said that the drought would end with rain on 23 August. Bickle was embarrassed in 1990 when a minister of another church in Kansas City produced metereological records showing above average rainfall for June 1983 (seven inches) and average rainfall in July that year. Bickle still defends the drought story although he has changed the explanation several times. A different version appears in his latest book.[11] Bickle still holds on to the contention that Jones is a prophet despite his moral failings and his occult connections because Jones gave divine validation to the so-called 'prophetic' ministry exercised by Kansas City Fellowship.

THE TURNING POINT

The publication of *Some Said it Thundered* and Wimber's promotion of the Kansas City prophets did immense harm in Britain by presenting a mixture of divination and personal prophecy as evidence of a fresh outpouring of the Holy Spirit. This caused great excitement among charismatics but it was a major diversion from the purposes of God. It was also a major turning point in the charismatic movement. It marked a shift away from a Bible-centred expression of the Holy Spirit working through the lives of ordinary believers in the church and paved the way for the next phase in the drift into experientialism and the acceptance of bizarre manifestations, exciting spiritual phenomena, non-biblical practices and extra-biblical revelation.

From that point in the summer and autumn of 1990 I believe that the charismatic movement actually became a stumbling-block to the gospel. The charismatic movement, which the pioneers in the early years had seen as restoring New Testament ministries and gifts to the church to enable her to fulfil her true prophetic function and save the nation, now became a hindrance to the fulfilment of those aims.

A major deception entered the church very publicly in 1990. It had, of course, been there in a latent form for a very long time. Its roots can be clearly seen in the Latter Rain movement, but it probably goes back much farther than that to earlier heresies. 1990 was a turning point for the British church because the deception was embraced by leaders – not just a few, but prominent leaders from mainline churches as well as from the house-church streams.

The great deception, albeit taken sincerely into the British churches through these leaders, was not simply the acceptance of the false prophecy about a great revival beginning that year, but the embracing of a whole package of false teaching. At the end of the Holy Trinity, Brompton conference for leaders led by John Wimber and the Kansas City prophets in July 1990 a statement was issued by a number of prominent leaders stating that they had examined the teaching and practice of the Kansas City prophets and they were fully satisfied with its correctness. This was despite the fact that one month earlier Kansas City Fellowship leaders had confessed to fifteen areas of error in their teaching and practice and there was no indication given of the way in which they had corrected those errors, neither had they had time to work through those corrections and to establish a firmer biblical base to their ministry.

APOSTLES AND PROPHETS

At the time of the July 1990 meetings I was not aware of the way John Wimber's ministry had been radically influenced by Bob Jones and Paul Cain. I had not then made a detailed study of their teaching. I subsequently listened to scores of their tapes and read numerous transcripts of their speeches and prophecies both at Anaheim and at Kansas City. Some of these prophecies have been recorded in Chapter Five. John Wimber's teaching, particularly at the Docklands Centre in October 1990, showed the extent to which he had embraced their teaching. He spoke about Joel's army, acknowledging that he had got the concept from Paul Cain and Bob Jones and saying that at first he had had difficulty in accepting it. From this one assumes that he must have recognised that the teaching he was giving was a complete reversal of Scripture. In the prophet Joel, the army of locusts is an army of judgment, but Jones and Wimber used it to say that the Lord was raising up an army of 'dread champions'. This term was one which Bob Jones had invented and has no scriptural foundation as was shown in Chapter Five. Central to Jones' scheme of 'end-times teaching' was the belief that God was raising up prophets and apostles. The prophets were to herald the way for the apostles who would govern the world.

Mike Bickle, speaking at John Wimber's church in Anaheim in 1989, referred to the apostolic authority that was being given to Wimber and the leadership of the Vineyard churches. God was raising up prophets and apostles among them who would be recognised by the whole church worldwide and through them God would give a new unity in the church under their governmental authority. This authority would be extended into the nations throughout the world. Prophets would be given the ability to know the secrets of men's hearts, to know what was being said in high places in Washington, Moscow and the capitals of the world. This revelation would give them enormous power which would enable the apostles to exercise their governmental authority to establish the Kingdom in preparation for the coming of Christ when they would present the Kingdom to him.

Bickle reported that on a number of occasions Bob Jones had prophesied,

> That the prophets had been emerging in the '80s and the office [had been increasing] in maturity, we're talking about the mature office of the prophet with full revelation, will be established in the '90s. . . . then the office of the apostle with full signs and wonders will emerge – you know, with Jesus Christ visiting them and commissioning them. You know how that the Lord appeared to the apostles, that kind of level of apostleship, with the signs and wonders of a true apostle 2 Cor 12:12, the full signs and wonders of Jesus, that will begin to take place after that.[12]

Bickle also reported that Paul Cain said that the Lord had spoken to him and told him that

> in the '90s when the office of the prophet is established across the nations with true revelation far beyond even what he is moving in right now, with revelation of the matters of state and government issues, and the secrets of men's hearts, beyond anything we have ever seen; he said when that becomes common in the body then their mission,

> . . . will be to build the altar for the apostles. They will go ahead and introduce and establish the apostles, in their place and then the apostles will have government.[13]

As Wimber did not deny or correct these statements given to his own congregation, we must therefore conclude that he accepted them. In fact these were not new thoughts for John Wimber. The prophets were confirming the conviction he had held for a number of years.

As far back as 1981, at the time Wimber assumed responsibility for the Vineyard group, he was already convinced that his mission was to lead an apostolic team with a worldwide ministry. He referred to it in the context of the mission given by Jesus to the apostles in the early church. He said, 'the Holy Spirit has put on my heart that I am going to take a group from my church, we'll be ministering in much the same way, we'll be going as an apostolic group. As an apostolic group there is power and anointing far beyond your normal ability to perform.'[14]

When Wimber came to Holy Trinity, Brompton in July 1990 he was convinced that when he returned to Britain in October he would see the start of the great revival which would sweep across Europe. He was so fully persuaded of this that he brought his whole family over from America to witness the great outpouring of supernatural power. This would launch him onto his divine mission of worldwide leadership. He believed that the Vineyard was the true model of the restored end-time church which he was divinely ordained to lead with his apostolic anointing.

When Wimber linked with Paul Cain and the Kansas City Fellowship he changed the emphasis of his ministry from signs and wonders in healing and evangelism to signs and wonders through prophetic revelation. The prophets would 'prophesy' that a church would join the 'new breed' and become part of the Vineyard fellowship. This often led to congregations being split. It was a practice which had caused deep resentment among the churches in Kansas City, but part of the Kansas City Fellowship's original vision was that there would be 'one church' in the city with one eldership serving under Mike Bickle, after Bickle submitted to Wimber's apostleship and the prophets reinforced and confirmed his authority. This fitted neatly with Wimber's own vision of the new unity coming into the restored church 'This 'one-city-one-church' concept had been the cause of complaints against John Wimber's ministry in the USA where his visits left a trail of division. Wimber would lead a three- or four-day teaching and celebration event in a city with the backing of several local pastors. As soon as the event was over the Vineyard would plant a congregation in the area and churches which had co-operated would lose members and pastors would feel betrayed.[15]

In Britain we were spared the division that assailed many churches in the USA, partly due to the strong warnings given in *Prophecy Today* which alerted many leaders to the dangers which were threatening to cross the Atlantic. Another decisive factor was the non-fulfilment of the predicted great revival. If there had been even the remotest sign of that prophecy being fulfilled, it is very probable that many charismatic churches in Britain would rapidly have come under Wimber's control.

CHURCH LEADERS' SUPPORT

Reference has already been made to the fact that a number of British church leaders rushed into print with a public statement issued in July 1990 supporting the Kansas City Fellowship ministry. The statement was issued from Holy Trinity, Brompton by Sandy Millar, probably in response to the articles in *Prophecy Today* which urged leaders to be on their guard and to test all these spiritual phenomena according to principles laid down in the New Testament. The statement gave unreserved support to the Kansas City prophets.

> We believe they are true servants of God, men of sound character, humility and evident integrity . . . We have no doubt about the validity of their ministry . . . and encourage as many as possible to attend the conferences to be held in Edinburgh, Harrogate and London in the autumn of this year, at which they will be ministering.[16]

The signatories included Gerald Coates (Pioneer), Graham Cray (St Michael-le-Belfry), Roger Forster (Ichthus), Lynn Green (YWAM), David McInnes (St Aldates, Oxford), Sandy Millar (Holy Trinity, Brompton), John Mumford (South West London Vineyard), David Pytches, Brian Skinner, Teddy Saunders, Barry Kissel (St Andrew's, Chorleywood), Terry Virgo (New Frontiers International), Ann Watson (widow of David Watson), Rick Williams (Riverside Vineyard, Teddington).

All had been 'ministered' to by the Kansas City Fellowship team. This was acknowledged in the statement they issued. The fact that they stated that they believed a man such as Bob Jones to be a 'true servant of God' and a man of 'sound character' is evidence of the extent to which they were deceived. It was the practice of the prophets led by Cain and Jones to give encouraging messages, supposedly from God, with promises of amazing power and greatly-expanded ministry. They were told they would be speaking to multitudes, seeing miracles, witnessing to kings and presidents and enjoying tremendous blessings. These prophecies resulted in bringing the recipients under the controlling spirit operated by the 'prophet'.

There are always serious consequences of believing false prophecy. It has a polluting effect upon the spiritual life of those who receive it. At best it is taking an alien *influence* into your life; at worst it is actually receiving an alien spirit. I have personal knowledge of several British church leaders who received false prophecies from Cain and Jones, believed them and then strove to fulfil them. The 'prophecy' thus exercised a controlling influence over the life of the recipient.

The 'use of prophetic gifting for controlling purposes' was tenth in the list of fifteen errors acknowledged by Kansas City Fellowship in May 1990,[17] but there is no evidence that they had abandoned the practice two months later (July 1990). The support of senior church leaders was essential if Wimber was to see the fulfilment of those things which the 'prophets' had predicted. He fully expected a mighty revival to break out in London in October. This had been prophesied by Cain whom he believed 'never got it wrong'. They had foretold the great revival would be accompanied by an explosion of signs and wonders leading to the submission of church leaders to Wimber's apostolic authority. He would also be given divine power over the enemies of the gospel to deal summarily with them in the same way as Peter dealt with Ananias and Sapphira. As the revival spread across the UK into continental Europe Wimber and his 'apostolic team' would assume governmental control of the nations.

All this had been prophesied by Cain and Jones and embraced by Wimber. It is doubtful if many of the

British leaders knew of Wimber's expectations, but their willing compliance played an important part in preparing the way for the October meetings. The prophecies of a great revival were repeated from many pulpits and anticipation was high.

PROMISES OF SUPERNATURAL POWER

The commendation of senior church leaders plus considerable publicity promising an exciting message and signs and wonders brought large crowds to the public meetings in Harrogate, Edinburgh and London in October 1990. Prominent British church leaders had endorsed this ministry, so the people lapped it up. Not being trained theologians, they looked to their pastors, ministers and priests to say whether or not the ministry was biblically respectable and should be heeded. Their ministers themselves were enthusiastically endorsing this new ministry and the message, so the people followed their leaders.

The amazing promises given at the Wimber meetings filled the people with excitement and anticipation. The teaching was a heady mixture drawn from bits of all the strange teachings that had run through the charismatic movement since the middle of the twentieth century – Latter Rain, Manifest Sons, Positive Confession, Signs and Wonders, Power Healing, Power Evangelism, Spiritual Warfare, New Breed and Joel's Army – to mention just a few. Elements of all these teachings came together in 1990 and were injected into the British church with great hype and all the charisma of American glamour ministries.

These strange teachings had been steadfastly resisted by most faithful preachers and Bible teachers in Britain for many years. But this latest onslaught was led by a man who was an excellent communicator, who appeared friendly, laidback and trustworthy. He was a man who had been commended by David Watson and a number of prominent Anglicans as well as denominational and house-church leaders. He came with a popular message attractively presented. This heady cocktail was drunk by leaders, pastors and elders in many of the British evangelical churches especially those in the charismatic sector.

The mainline churches in Britain were particularly vulnerable due to the years of decline. In fact the whole nation was labouring under a cloud of status deprivation from loss of Empire and world prestige. Here was a message of hope. Here was a message of power to the powerless. Here was a message of light and life to scatter the darkness of moribund inactivity. But the promises were false. This was partially acknowledged by John Wimber at Holy Trinity, Brompton in June 1991 and again at the New Wine conference in August 1995. What has never been recognised, however, is the extent to which these promises were rooted in false teaching.

The foundation of this teaching lay in the belief that in the last days there would be a mighty outpouring of the Holy Spirit empowering the saints to perform great signs and wonders. Some of this teaching was based upon prophetic revelation which Bob Jones claimed to have been given by the Holy Spirit. He said that the 'last generation' would be those born since 1973 and that they would be an elect company of believers of the seed of the apostles. They would be 'omega children'. Jesus was the 'Alpha' and they are the 'Omega'. Jesus inaugurated the Kingdom, and the elect company of omega believers would complete the work and establish a glorious church on earth reigning over the nations.[18]

This teaching, which was given by both Jones and Cain, became the basis of the Vineyard/Kansas City Fellowship revivalist preaching. But it has no biblical foundation. The Bible declares Jesus to be both 'Alpha and Omega' (Rev 21:6). New Testament eschatology says that Jesus will come again to complete the work of the Kingdom. The Father will not take this away from his Son and entrust it to human hands.

There is a great need today to study what the Bible actually says about the Kingdom of God and the Second Coming of Christ. This may, in fact, provide the key to bringing the charismatic movement back onto a firm biblical basis. In Matthew 24 Jesus gave a series of signs of the end of the age, none of which promised supernatural power to believers. He warned those who are his followers to be alert to resist deception; to expect false christs, wars and rumours of wars, famines and earthquakes, persecution, apostasy, betrayal, false prophets, the increase of wickedness and a lack of love within the church. He nevertheless promised that the 'gospel of the kingdom will be preached in the whole world' (v 14). The only prediction of supernatural power was in an additional warning about deception!

> 'For false christs and false prophets will appear and perform great signs and miracles to deceive even the elect – if that were possible'.
>
> (v 24)

This is not the only warning in the New Testament concerning deception in the last days. Paul spoke of a time of great lawlessness which, he said, 'will be in accordance with the work of Satan displayed in all kinds of counterfeit miracles, signs and wonders' (2 Thess 2:9); and writing to Timothy he warned,

> the time will come when men will not put up with

> sound doctrine. Instead, to suit their own desires, they will gather around them a great number of teachers to say what their itching ears want to hear. They will turn their ears away from the truth and turn aside to myths.
>
> (2 Tim 4:3–4)

These warnings and a number of others, are in the New Testament for our own protection so that we will be alert to the intentions of the enemy to deceive, and to the strategy which may be employed. This is where a knowledge of the Bible is essential. When we move away from Scripture and invent doctrine, however attractive, we are in grave danger of deception. Once we are loosed from the Word of God we are adrift on the high seas like a rudderless ship in a storm.

NON-BIBLICAL TEACHING

The injection into the British church in 1990 of a package of non-biblical teaching promising supernatural power, signs and wonders and imminent revival, marked a milestone in the apostatising of the charismatic movement in Britain. The way had been prepared for this by a gradual and almost imperceptible down-grading of the Bible from its place of centrality within the Protestant tradition. This could be seen in the increasing separation between the reading and exposition of the Word of God, and the exercise of spiritual gifts. Jesus was perfectly clear in stating that signs and wonders would *follow* the preaching of the Word. This is what happens in the poorer non-industrial nations, where multitudes have been coming to Christ throughout the second half of this century. At large gatherings where the Word of God is proclaimed, while the preacher is still speaking miraculous healings occur, many are born again and the signs and wonders of the presence of God through the work of the Holy Spirit is evident.[19]

In charismatic churches in the western nations, by contrast, we have developed the practice of separating Word and Spirit. When we reach the end of our act of worship, or service, where there has been singing, prayer and the exposition of the Word, then we clear away the chairs or invite people forward saying 'Now we'll have a time of ministry!' Over the years these so called 'ministry times' have gone from the simple praying for the sick to the performance of all kinds of bizarre manifestations as we have moved farther and farther away from a biblical centre.

Peter Fenwick, in Chapter Three, has shown how the path to the Kansas City Fellowship 1990 package had been well prepared by Restorationist teaching – at least in the house-church streams. The new factor was the open door into the mainline churches which enabled their teaching to sweep right through the denominations. This was very largely due to John Wimber's acceptability, which in turn, had been due to David Watson's influence and subsequently to the support of several influential Anglican clergy.

A number of prominent charismatic leaders also embraced the false teachings presented in 1990. They were on an escalator from which there was no turning back and which it was not easy to jump off without risking personal injury. Their reputations were at stake and they had taken false promises into their spiritual lives. Many of them also took into their teaching and preaching the false expectations of a great revival. Churches such as St Andrew's, Chorleywood gave great prominence to preparing the congregation for revival and for the expected inflow of large numbers of new believers. But the revival did not happen.

By 1994 it was becoming difficult to sustain the enthusiasm of the people and to stave off massive disillusionment. The credibility of leaders was on the line. The Toronto Blessing arrived just in time to provide a new wave of excitement. With its coming, many leaders cut down or even abandoned the preaching of the Word in order to get into the 'ministry time' as quickly as possible. Thus the move of many charismatic churches into experience-centred phenomena took another leap forward. But the way had been prepared by twenty-five years of neglect of the Bible and a lack of biblical scholarship among charismatic leaders, which left an open door for the Toronto Blessing.

The eagerness with which Toronto was embraced is an indication of a deep spiritual hunger and a longing for God to 'rend the heavens and come down' and bring a mighty revival to transform the decaying life of the western nations. But even this longing for revival is a reflection of the values of the world where the whole of our society is looking for 'quick fix' solutions to all our problems. In the church we are not prepared for the cost of obeying the 'Great Commission' and 'making disciples, teaching them to obey' everything the Lord has taught us (Matt 28:19–20). Instead, we look for supernatural power to create an instant, ready-made reproduction model.

It is this human longing for revival that has opened the way for many of the strange things which have become associated with the charismatic churches over the years. This eagerness to see the reign of God on earth and to promote the work of the Kingdom is surely good. But in the western nations generally the Bible has been abandoned. Humanistic and New Age teachings have been widely embraced in a increasingly secularised post-Christian society and the churches, especially charismatics, have been influenced more then we realise.

Many evangelicals, especially those who have embraced the charismata, have tended to follow the world in neglecting the systematic study of the Bible and whole-hearted commitment to its teaching and living according to its moral and spiritual precepts. We have elevated spiritual excitement to new heights leaving the door open for non-biblical teaching and lax standards of personal and corporate morality.

Of course this is a generalisation and we would not wish to imply that there are no faithful evangelicals who love the Word of God and live godly lives. Neither would we wish to imply that none of those in churches affected by the Toronto Blessing have been blessed by God. As Peter Fenwick has clearly stated in Chapter Three, God will always honour those who come to him with clean hands and a pure heart, or with humility and repentance. God longs to bless his children and those who come in sincerity will not go away empty-handed. I personally know many believers who have been blessed by attending 'Toronto' meetings. But this is evidence of the faithfulness of our God who loves to bless his children. It is certainly not an endorsement of the Toronto Blessing. God does not initiate things which are contrary to his own word in Scripture.

There is, nevertheless, cause for concern regarding this new wave of excitement which swept through the charismatic churches in 1994 and 1995. It has not brought revival, neither will it even prepare the way for revival. It has proved to be yet another blind alley that has actually led the church away from fulfilling the purposes of God. There is also cause for concern that, as the charismatic movement increasingly embraces the experiential, the way is open for even more bizarre behavioural phenomena and the embracing of heretical New Age type teachings and practices. Once the Toronto Blessing disappears from the churches what will be the next wave to be introduced?

A MOVE OF GOD?

Having reached this point in the review of the development of the charismatic movement we may return to the question posed in Chapter Two. Is the charismatic movement a move of God? Was it initiated by the Lord Jesus? Despite all the strange aberrations we have noted, I would still want to affirm very positively its divine origins. I could not deny the work of the Holy Spirit in my own life or in the many hundreds of churches of which I have personal experience. Through what we call the charismatic movement, the Holy Spirit has brought new life, joy, liberty and a more intimate personal relationship with the Lord Jesus and the Father into the lives of millions of believers. This has to be the work of God. It is certainly not anything that Satan would want to do.

The fact that the charismatic movement had no clear-cut beginning causes me to doubt that God has moved in a series of 'waves' at different points during the twentieth century. I see a continuous process in the work of the Holy Spirit throughout the century. On the first day of 1900, Charles Parnham's students began speaking in tongues, this was followed in 1906 by the stirring events in Azusa Street resulting in the formation of Pentecostal assemblies.

Gradually throughout the century the recognition of the presence and power of the Holy Spirit has spread across the world. This has brought spiritual awakening in lands where the gospel had never previously been heard, with vast numbers of new-born believers. It has also brought spiritual renewal in nations that had had the gospel for centuries and where the church had become largely inactive due to the onslaught of secularisation. It was clearly God's intention to reap a mighty harvest during this century in lands which had never before been reached by the gospel and it was also clearly his intention to renew the flagging belief and spiritual power of the church where institutionalism and traditionalism had sapped its strength. What we see as fresh 'waves' of the Spirit have in fact been part of the on-going work of the Spirit of God working out his purposes and preparing a great company of believers to withstand the stormy days that lie ahead.

USING HUMAN STRENGTH

The great failing of the charismatic movement has not been in a lack of enthusiasm but in taking over the work of God and trying to do that work in our own strength. It is recorded that Frank Bartlemann, the Azusa Street leader, said that within a few years of the 1906 experience the flesh had taken over from the Spirit. This is really what has happened to the charismatic movement over the past twenty-five years. Paul's warning to the church in Galatia needs to be heeded today, 'After beginning with the Spirit, are you now trying to attain your goal by human effort?' (Gal 3: 3).

There are many indications that we have done something similar to the offence caused by Aaron's sons, Nadab and Abihu, who put unauthorised fire ('strange fire' AV) in their censers which they then offered before the Lord with disastrous results (Lev 10:1). When we do such things we are showing a lack of trust in the Lord. We are trying to force the pace and direct the work of God. Once we begin to move in the flesh and not under the direction and in the power of the Holy Spirit we open the door to all kinds of alien influences as well as to the things of the flesh such as pride and arrogance. When we take over the work of God we are, in fact, rebelling against him and we grieve the Holy Spirit. Isaiah 63:10 speaks of the terrible consequences of such action, 'In his love and mercy he redeemed them . . . Yet they rebelled and grieved his Holy Spirit. So he turned and became their enemy and he himself fought against them.'

This needs to be taken as a serious warning by all who are part of the charismatic movement. If we seriously step outside the will of the Lord he is against us, not for us. It is essential that we should understand both the will of God and his ways because all the evidence points to the fact that the world is moving closer and closer into days of international turmoil and conflict. The moral and spiritual plight of the nations, especially in the West, is desperate. But God is actually using this social situation to prepare the way for the gospel. Never has there been a greater need for the Word of God to be clearly heard among the nations. Never has there been a greater need for the establishment of biblical principles as the guidelines for healthy living both for individuals and at a corporate level. Yet the influence of the church in the western nations has never been so weak.

In Britain the church is under continuous attack from the media who delight to scorn the gospel and seize every opportunity to mock the faith. The Church of England, as the established church, holds a unique position which is rapidly being eroded by unbelief and by spiritual and moral corruption from within. It was obvious to all those who were aware of the tactics of the enemy that as soon as the issue of women priests was over, the next battle would be over the acceptance of homosexual priests, both men and women. When that battle is over the way will be prepared for the ultimate onslaught on biblical belief from the multi-faith lobby.

BATTLE FOR THE BIBLE

As Peter Fenwick has rightly said, in Chapter Three, the real battle today is a battle for the Bible; it is a battle for the soul of Britain. Alongside the battle within the church and the attacks of a secular media, there is the growing power of Islam. The Muslims are determined to make Britain the first Islamic state in Europe. They have been planting mosques in all the towns and cities of Britain at the rate of one per month since the mid-1980s.

During the 1990s Britain has celebrated the 50th anniversary of the Battle of Britain and the war in Europe. That was a battle for physical survival. The battle today is for spiritual survival. The Holy Spirit whom God began to pour out upon all believers on the Day of Pentecost is still active in the world today. As the battle against the enemies of the gospel intensifies there is a new urgency that the church should recognise the nature of the battle and understand the reasons why Jesus, shortly before his ascension, told the disciples, 'Do not leave Jerusalem, but wait for the gift my Father promised . . . you will receive power when the Holy Spirit comes on you' (Acts 1: 4–8).

Jesus knew that without the power of the Holy Spirit his followers would not be able to withstand the attacks of the enemy. They had to learn not to rush out in human enthusiasm or to seek after exciting signs and wonders but faithfully to be witnesses of the Lord Jesus, declaring the way of salvation to all those around them and trusting the Lord of the harvest to bring forth the fruit of the Spirit and enlarge his Kingdom until the Day of the Lord dawns.

WHERE TOMORROW?

We began this book by saying that the charismatic movement had reached a point beyond crisis and is already beginning to crumble. In Britain there is a significant number of ministers who were once exercising charismatic ministries and who today repudiate that term. There are thousands of church members who have left charismatic churches because they have been sickened by the behaviour of leaders who, under the influence of Toronto, each time they began to read Scripture or preach the Word became doubled up as with stomach cramp and fell to the ground in a helpless heap. They were sickened by being told that uncontrollable laughter, barking, roaring, mooing, crowing like a cockerel, shouting, screaming, vomiting, pogo dancing and shadow boxing are all signs of the activity of the Holy Spirit.

They remembered that these same leaders who encouraged these things were saying, only a few years ago, that such activities were clear evidence of the presence of demonic spirits and required deliverance. They have been saddened to see the Holy Spirit ridiculed in TV programmes and tabloid press reports by displays of bizarre activity. They have been dismayed to see the name of the Lord Jesus mocked in the media through the activities of some charismatics.

There are those who, like the authors of this book, still hold fast to their belief in the charismata. They believe that the Holy Spirit is present and active among believers today as he was in the days of the early church and that the gifts of the Spirit are available to all believers. They nevertheless believe that after more than twenty-five years of the charismatic movement in Britain it is right to ask some fundamental questions concerning our response to the work of the Spirit among us. If, as we believe, it was God's purpose to renew the church and revive the nation, has that purpose been achieved? There is no evidence to suggest that the spiritual life of the whole church has been revitalised and neither is there any evidence of moral or spiritual revival in the nation. Indeed, the moral and spiritual life of both church and nation are infinitely worse. Scandals concerning adultery, homosexuality and child abuse are regularly revealed – and that's only within the church! In the nation all these things occur plus violence, murder and all kinds of corruption.

So what has gone wrong? The plain and simple answer is that we have turned our back upon the Word of God. We have neglected to study the Word, we have relegated it to a secondary place in the life of the church and we have substituted experience, false prophecies, strange revelations, our own opinions and teachings. We have thereby abandoned the truth for the myths and fantasies and teachings of men. We are today reaping the inevitable reward of the tares that have been sown among us. Although many people are still enjoying the exciting experiences of the latest wave of charismatic chaos, I believe the outlook for the future of the charismatic movement is bleak, the writing is already upon the wall.

I believe future church historians will see 1990 as the major turning point in the apostatising of the charismatic movement. This was the time when all the strange, unbiblical teachings which had been current among Pentecostal/charismatics since the Latter Rain Revival of the 1940s were gathered into a complete package and swallowed uncritically by the church in Britain. Foremost in the body of this teaching was the expectation of a great revival brought about by signs and wonders. There is no scriptural foundation for such a belief. Indeed, Jesus did not use signs and wonders to astound the crowds and draw them into Kingdom. Quite the reverse, he instructed people whom he had healed to keep quiet about it, not to 'noise it abroad'. The New Testament teaches that signs and wonders *follow* the preaching of the Word, but once we start making the miraculous the chief object of desire, once we start running after signs and wonders, we take the focus away from the centrality of the Word of God and the glorifying of the Lord Jesus.

A major problem for us in the West has been the amazing growth of the church in the poor non-industrialised nations of the world. In these days of easy travel and rapid communications, many church leaders have been to the poorer nations and seen at first hand what is happening. They have returned with accounts of multitudes being saved at great open air meetings with amazing miracles – the blind seeing, the deaf hearing, the lame walking and even the dead being raised. I myself have seen evidence of all these things in my preaching travels across Africa, China, South East Asia and other parts of the world. I too have brought these stories back and used them to make westerners jealous by saying that the same things could and should be happening here. These stories have fuelled the longing for revival.

What has happened in Britain has also happened in other western nations; the deep desire for revival has caused us to run ahead of the timing of the Lord. God has been telling us for many years that he is 'shaking the nations' and that his purpose is to turn the hearts of men and women away from their trust in material things, which is idolatry, to seeking first the Kingdom of God and his righteousness. In the highly secularised, materialistic western industrialised nations our whole culture revolves around the acquisition of wealth and the accumulation of material possessions. These things largely determine our position in society and they therefore have a far greater influence upon our values and our mindset than most of us realise. It is almost impossible to divorce ourselves from the culture of the society in which we live.

A CULTURE OF IDOLATRY

There is no place in our culture for the God of the Bible; the God who demands our total loyalty and our absolute trust. The western culture is a culture of idolatry and we are adherents, willingly or unwillingly, of that culture. There will be no revival until that idolatrous mindset is broken in the servants of God. That is why revivals and great spiritual awakenings have always occurred among the poor and the underprivileged, from the days of the early church to the impoverished nations of today. Soon after the Day of Pentecost, as revival swept through the city of Jerusalem, the rich and the powerful noted with scorn that the apostles were unlearned men, they 'realised that they were unschooled, ordinary men, they were astonished and they took note that these men had been with Jesus' (Acts 4:13).

The same is true of those who came to Christ in the Wesleyan revival, of the blacks and poor whites who flocked to Azusa Street in 1906 and of the revival that swept through the Welsh mining communities in the same decade.

In the rich western nations evangelicals have become obsessed with revival and the desire to reproduce what is happening in the poorer nations. What we fail to realise is the vast cultural difference and we cannot compensate for this simply by greater enthusiasm or by turning up the volume of our praise and worship, or even by more earnest intercession. Even confession, repentance, weeping and crying out to God at our meetings will not provide the quick-fix answer for which we are looking and which our quick-fix culture moulds our mindset to expect.

THE KEY TO REVIVAL

The key to revival is in Philippians 3:7–10 where Paul describes how he has renounced the world for the sake of knowing Christ Jesus as his Lord. He considers all worldly values as rubbish so that he may gain – not the gifts of the Holy Spirit, or supernatural power to confound unbelievers – but simply that he may 'gain Christ and be found in him'. He says, 'I want to know Christ and the power of his resurrection.' In case anyone should interpret this to mean an exciting experience of having the power to raise the dead, Paul's next words should be noted! He adds, 'and the fellowship of sharing in his sufferings, becoming like him in his death.' The way to life is through death; death to self and the renunciation of the world. There is no other way for the church in the western nations to see revival. It may be part of God's plan to allow the church in the rich industrial nations to die in order to raise a new and purified church.

The great spiritual awakenings in the poorer nations are not being seen in the West because we are unwilling to meet the cost. We want the excitement of revival without paying the price of the pain and suffering and travail that goes with it. In the poorer nations the great spiritual awakenings are occurring because the gospel of salvation is being preached, the good news that Christ died for our sins. Multitudes are being saved and the signs and wonders follow. This has been the pattern in past revivals. But in the western charismatic churches we are not motivated by the desire to save multitudes going to hell but to have the multitudes come and join us in the excitement of a spiritual spectacular! If they won't come and join us then we'll have it on our own! Furthermore, if God won't do it for us, then we'll do it ourselves!

This is the tragedy of the western charismatic movement. We are children of the world rather than the children of God. Our lifestyle is very little different from our unbelieving neighbours; our values are similar to theirs; we read the same newspapers, watch the same TV programmes, follow the same fashions in clothes, food and music; even our charismatic worship sometimes sounds more like a pop concert. We justify this by saying that it helps modern people to feel comfortable and at home in our midst; in other words, that they haven't had to leave the world in order to come into the church! How different from New Testament teaching! How different from the teaching of the Reformers and the Great Revivalist preachers.

The church in the poor non-industrialised nations is presently thriving and expanding rapidly but there is great danger of spiritual pollution from the West. In these days of worldwide travel and communications the materialistic values of the West may be easily transmitted, especially in the context of the western nations' economic power and dominance.

Here is a parable. In the early 1980s a West African preacher of extraordinary gifting arose out of a background of grinding poverty. He had an anointed ministry of evangelism and began drawing crowds of up to half a million at his rallies. Thousands responded to the gospel giving their lives to Christ and as they did so there were miraculous healings and many other signs and wonders which were reported in the secular press. Soon some westerners got to hear of his ministry and took him on a tour around the rich nations. They poured money into his lap. They taught him the 'prosperity gospel' by which they lived and convinced him that God wanted him rich as a sign to the poor Africans among whom he ministered. He built a great church building; he also built himself a fine home and rode around in a chauffeur-driven Mercedes. He became a great man in his community but he lost his anointing. His ministry of evangelism disappeared.

LOOKING AHEAD

If the charismatic movement is to fulfil the purposes of God there has to be, first of all, a recognition that things have gone radically wrong and of the reasons why this has happened. There has to be not merely a superficial repentance but a radical turning away from the world and returning to God. The Bible has to be restored to its central place in the church with serious study of the Word of God given great importance not only among leaders and preachers of the Word but in the lives of all believers. If this does not take place there will be serious consequences for the whole church in the western nations. The likely consequences may be summarised under four headings.

Disintegration

The charismatic movement is likely to disintegrate and fragment into numerous small groups with different beliefs and emphases. As the movement becomes largely discredited many people will leave charismatic churches and revert to traditional evangelicalism or other traditions or even leave the church altogether.

Experientialism

If the present obsession with experience continues, the charismatic movement will produce a new wave of excitement in two or three years time just as it has done every few years over the past fifteen years. With the abandonment of the Bible as the sole criterion of truth, each new wave takes the charismatic movement farther away from New Testament Christianity. The danger becomes increased of a drift into the New Age Movement or to becoming cults. Both of these aberrations are basically experiential.

Timing

The fresh outpouring of the Holy Spirit in the twentieth century that has resulted first in the Pentecostal movement and secondly in the charismatic movement has been part of the deliberate plan and purpose of God for these times; empowering his church for the demands of the coming days. God has not left us without an understanding of his plans. For a number of years he has been speaking to us about shaking the nations but we have not listened with understanding, neither have we been content to allow him to work out his purposes and to await his timing. Instead of waiting for God to do the work of revival in the nation, we have rushed ahead. Like the Children of Israel in the wilderness when Moses was up the mountain, we have made our own golden calf which we have worshipped in the charismatic churches.

By the beginning of 1995 the shaking of the nations had reached the point where the conditions for revival were falling into place. This was certainly true in Britain where a combination of deep social malaise, economic problems and political uncertainty combined to shake the confidence of the nation. Even the monarchy, heart of the British establishment, appeared deeply wounded by its '*annus horribilis*'.

The charismatic movement had been raised by God for just such a time as this. Instead of witnessing to the nation, however, the charismatic churches turned in upon themselves, enjoying their golden calf, but thereby rendering themselves incapable of bringing the Word of God to the nation with power and authority.

These social conditions in the nation which are favourable to the gospel are unlikely to last long and the window of opportunity will close. Days of darkness are likely to follow with the enemies of the gospel multiplying and the church growing weaker. The visitation of God will have been missed, as it was in New Testament times. It was this that caused Jesus to weep over the city of Jerusalem saying,

> 'If you, even you, had only known on this day what would bring you peace – but now it is hidden from your eyes . . . your enemies will build an embankment against you . . . They will not leave one stone on another, because you did not recognise the time of God's coming to you.'
>
> (Luke 19:41–44).

A stumbling-block

Missing the timing of God does not necessarily mean that his purposes will be blocked. The sovereignty of God ensures that he will carry out his purposes even if his people are unfaithful. He will work out his plans another way. In the time of Jeremiah he had to abandon Judah, allowing Jerusalem and the Temple to be destroyed because of the wickedness and unresponsiveness of his people despite all the warnings that he sent to them.

The purposes of God, however, cannot be thwarted. The sovereignty of God ensures that he can fulfil his plans by other means. As John the Baptist declared, 'I tell you that out of these stones God can raise up children for Abraham' (Luke 3:8).

If there is no repentance among charismatics and no radical renewing of the western church God is able to fulfil his purposes by other means. It may be that he will by-pass the church and bring salvation to the nation some other way. Indeed it may well happen that God will allow the western church to disintegrate. As the church in the West dies so he will raise up the church in the East and in the poorer nations to be his servants and to bring the message of salvation to the world. This would be completely in line with the ways of God in Scripture and a fulfilment of the vision Mary saw after her visit to Elizabeth when she looked forward to the birth of the Saviour singing,

> 'My soul glorifies the Lord
>   and my spirit rejoices in God my Saviour,
> for he has been mindful of the humble state of
>   his servant . . .
> He has brought down rulers from their thrones
>   but has lifted up the humble.
> He has filled the hungry with good things
>   but has sent the rich away empty.'
>
> (Luke 1: 46–53)

Conclusion

It would not be right to end on a negative note, although I would not wish to lessen the impact of the solemn warnings given in this chapter. But our God is merciful and loving, very ready to forgive and to restore those who turn to him in penitence.

It is the earnest hope of the writers of this book that our brothers and sisters in Christ, especially those with leadership responsibilities within the churches, will respond to the things we have written by examining their teaching and practices in the light of Scripture. We appeal to the whole church, and especially those in the charismatic sector, to make a fresh commitment to the study of the Word of God. We believe there is a pressing need for the study of biblical eschatology to counter the many false teachings which abound today. It is essential that Christians should know what the Bible says about the Second Coming of Christ and the conditions leading up to the Parousia.

We therefore appeal to all preachers to undertake systematic expository preaching of the Word of God. We believe that expounding the Scriptures will undoubtedly lay a good foundation for spiritual revival in the nation, but it will also guard the church against error in days where there is a great onslaught on the truth. If believers are well-grounded in the Word, they will not be deceived by false teachers and prophets however attractively their message is packaged and presented.

We appeal also to all believers to turn again to the Bible and study the Word. When we do so we find our love for God grows and so too does our commitment to the Lord Jesus and to the work of the Kingdom.

To those who, having read this book, are concerned about their own spiritual life if they have been exposed to non-biblical teaching and practices, we would counsel against anxiety. Our God is a loving Father who sees the heart rather than the outward appearance (1 Sam 16: 7). He knows the secrets of our hearts and he guards those who sincerely love him and who truly seek him. His solemn promise is ' "You will seek me and find me when you seek me with all your heart. I will be found by you," declares the Lord' (Jer 29: 13–14).

Those who have been saved by the precious blood of the Lord Jesus are part of his flock whom he, as the Good Shepherd, guards and constantly watches over for good. Even when we foolishly or inadvertently go astray he is not quick to condemn, but rather he is quick to reach out to redeem, and lovingly to restore to a right relationship with himself and with the Father.

Making mistakes, repenting and returning to experiencing the loving forgiveness of our Father are all part of growing in maturity for the believer. There is no one who never makes mistakes. We all go astray from time to time, but our God remains faithful, even when we are unfaithful. He has called us his children, sons of the living God, and the Father has fulfilled his promise to send 'the Counsellor' to be with us for every – 'the Spirit of truth' (John 14: 16–17). Jesus promised that 'the Counsellor, the Holy Spirit . . . will teach you all things and will remind you of everything I have said to you . . . Do not let your hearts be troubled and do not be afraid' (John 14: 26–27).

Jesus' own testimony was that he only did those things which he heard from the Father (John 5: 19). He said, 'By myself I can do nothing' (John 5: 30). It is this attitude of total dependence upon the Father that the whole church urgently needs to learn, so that we neither lag behind nor run ahead of his purposes. If we turn to the left or to the right we hear his voice saying 'This is the way, walk in it' (Is. 30: 21).

When we study the Word of God we learn his ways. He sometimes has to bring a loving rebuke to us, 'I am the Lord your God, who teaches you what is best for you, who directs you in the way you should go. If only you had paid attention to my commands, your peace would have been like a river' (Is 48: 17–18).

Yet he also promises full restoration to those who humbly return to him. '"Though the mountains be shaken and the hills be removed, yet my unfailing love for you will not be shaken nor my covenant of peace be removed," says the Lord who has compassion on you' (Is 54: 10).

Notes

Chapter One

1. Hank Hanegraaff, *Christianity in Crisis* (Eugene, Oregon, Harvest House Publishers, 1993).
2. *The World Christian Encyclopedia*, ed. David Barrett (Overseas Ministries Study Center, 490 Prospect St., Newhaven, Connecticut, 06511, USA, updated each January by International Bulletin of Missionary Research, 1966).

Chapter Two

1. David Lillie, *God-centred Communities in a Man-centred World*, published by the author, Lark Rise, Mill Lane, Exton, nr Exeter, EX3 0PH.
2. John Wimber, quoted in *Today* magazine, 24.8.95.

Chapter 4

1. Richard M. Riss, *Latter Rain* (Honeycomb Visual Productions Ltd., Ontario, 1987) p 55.
2. Ibid pp 55–56.
3. A. J. Dager, *Vengeance is Ours* (Sword Publishers, Washington, 1990) p 49.
4. Franklin Hall, *Atomic Power with God Through Fasting and Prayer* (Hall Deliverance Foundation, Phoenix, 1975) p 19.
5. Franklin Hall, Newsletter 'Miracle Word' (Hall Deliverance Foundation, 1985) p 10.
6. Franklin Hall, *The Return of Immortality* (Hall Deliverance Foundation, 1976) p 60.
7. Ibid p 3.
8. Ibid p 3.

9. Richard M. Riss, *Latter Rain*, p 56.
10. Pearry Green, *The Acts of the Prophet* (Tuscon Tabernacle Books, Tuscon) p 39.
11. Ibid p 40.
12. William M. Branham, *An Exposition of the Seven Church Ages* (Spoken Word Publications Jeffersonville, 1984) p 321.
13. Ibid p 322.
14. Pearry Green, *The Acts of the Prophet*, p 69.
15. Ibid p 70.
16. A. J. Dager, *Vengeance is Ours*, p 57.
17. David E. Harrell Jr., *All Things are Possible* (Indiana Univ. Press, Bloomington, 1975) pp 35–36.
18. Walter J. Hollenweger, *The Pentecostals* (Augsburg Publishing House, Minneapolis, 1972) pp 354–355.
19. Clifford Hill, 'Kansas City Prophets', *Prophecy Today* (London, July/August, 1990) p 6.
20. David E. Harrell Jr., *All Things are Possible*, p 161.
21. Richard M. Riss, *Latter Rain*, p 51.
22. Ibid p 58.
23. Ibid p 60.
24. G. Warnock, *The Feast of Tabernacles* (Sharon Publishers, N. Battleford, 1951) pp 3–4.
25. Richard M. Riss, *Latter Rain*, p 70.
26. Ibid p 74.
27. G. Warnock, *The Feast of Tabernacles*, p 3.
28. Richard M. Riss, *Latter Rain*, p 74.
29. Ibid p 95.
30. James A. Watt, 'A Historical Analysis of the Development of Two Concepts of "Presbytery" ' (James A. Watt, Seattle, 1972) p 4.
31. Bill Britton, *The Branch* (Bill Britton, Springfield) p 4.
32. Ernst A. Gruen, 'Documenation of the Aberrant Practices and Teachings of Kansas City Fellowship' (Full Faith Church of Love, Kansas City, 1990).
33. Dr Jack Deere, 'Joel's Army' (Audio tape message, 1990).
34. Ernest A. Gruen, 'Documentation', p 218.
35. Ibid p 10.
36. Ibid p 12.

37. Marc Dupont, *1994: The Year of the Lion* (Mantle of Praise Ministries Inc., Mississuaga, 1994) pp 1–2.
38. Ibid p 3.
39. Randy Clark, 'A Prophetic Foundation' (audio tape message, 1995).

Chapter Five

1. Published in *New Covenant*; Charismatic Renewal Services, Ann Arbor, Michigan 48107, USA) February 1978, p 4.
2. Ibid p 5.
3. Ibid p 6.
4. I am indebted to Patricia Higton of *Time Ministries International*, Emmanuel Church, Hawkwell, Essex, SS5 4NR for the record of this prophecy.
5. Ibid.
6. *Prophecy Today*, published by PWM Trust, The Park, Moggerhanger, Bedford, MK44 3RW. Published in each edition of *Prophecy Today* since March 1984.
7. *Prophecy Today* Vol 10 No 4, July/Aug 94.
8. *Prophecy Today* Vol 2 No 4, July/Aug 86.
9. This prophecy was given by David Minor on 6 April 1987.
10. Rick Joiner, *The Harvest* (1989). Distributed by Morning Star Publications Inc., Charlotte, N. Carolina, 28226, USA.
11. David Pytches, *Some Said It Thundered* (London, Hodders, 1990) p 52.
12. 'Introducing the Prophetic Ministry', article by John Wimber in *Equipping the Saints*, special UK edition/ Fall 1990, Vineyard Ministries International, PO Box 163, London, SW20 813X.
13. Ibid pp 5–6.
14. Paul Cain, *A New Breed of Man*, Kevin Springer; ibid p 12.
15. Paul Cain, speaking at 'School of Prophecy', Anaheim, California, USA, Vineyard Ministries International, November 1989; transcript of tapes published by Holly Assembly of God, 104 Lake Street, Holly, M1 48442; Session 7, Part 1, p 6.

16. Ibid p 7.
17. Ibid p 7.
18. Ibid Session 7, Part II, p 1.
19. Ibid p 9.
20. Ibid p 14.
21. Leaflet issued by Vintage Ministries, 41a South Clerk Street, Edinburgh, EH8 9NZ.
22. Ibid.
23. Paul Cain, 'School of Prophecy' op cit p 9.
24. Ibid p 9.
25. Ibid p 11.
26. Ibid p 15.
27. Ibid p 19.
28. Ibid p 21.
29. Ibid p 21.
30. Colin Urquhart, Newsletter published by Kingdom Faith Ministries, National Revival Centre, Roffey Place, Horsham, W. Sussex.
31. 'Latter Day Prophets' a special report by Albert Dager in *Media Spotlight*: a Biblical Analysis of religious and Secular Media, PO Box 290 Redmont, WA 98073, USA, October 1990.

Chapter Seven

1. Quoted in *Rich Christians, Poor Christians* Monica Hill (London, Marshall Pickering 1989), p 2. These figures are updated annually in *International Bulletin of Missionary Research*, 490 Prospect Street, New Haven, Connecticut 06511, USA.
2. See Monica Hill, *Rich Christians, Poor Christians* (London, Marshall Pickering, 1989) p 60f.
3. See *Shaking the Nations*, Clifford Hill (Eastbourne, Kingsway, 1995).
4. Reported by Rick Williams at a clergy conference in St Andrew's Chorleywood, 7 March 1990, transcription of tape.
5. *Prophecy Today*, Vol 6 No 4.
6. David Pytches *Some said it Thundered* (London, Hodders, 1990), p 27.
7. Ibid p 16.

8. Vineyard Ministries School of Prophecy, Anaheim 1989, Bob Jones, transcript of tape, 20.
9. Matthew 18 is often wrongly applied. Originally it was meant to apply to situations within a local church fellowship. Moreover it deals with *sin* in personal relationships. It was never intended to apply to disputes over teaching and practice, or with any doctrinal issues. Both Paul and John did not hesitate to name those whom they judged to be false teachers and whose doctrine was deviating from the truth and thereby harming the church.
10. *Prophecy Today*, Vol 6 No 4, July 1990.
11. Mike Bickle, *Growing in the Prophetic* (Eastbourne, Kingsway, 1995).
12. Vineyard Ministries School of Prophecy, Anaheim 1989, transcript of tape, p 10.
13. Ibid.
14. John Wimber, Healing Seminar Series, audio tapes, 1981, quoted in 'Testing the Fruit of the Vineyard' *Media Spotlight*, PO Box 290, Redmond, WA 98073-0290.
15. James R. Loggins and Paul G. Hiebert, quoted in Latter Day Prophets, *Media Spotlight*, op. cit.
16. Published in *Renewal*, October 1990.
17. Published in *Prophecy Today*, Vol 6 No 5, September 1990.
18. Vineyard School of Prophecy, Bob Jones, op cit. p 1.
19. See *Prophecy Today* Vol 1 No 3 July 1985.